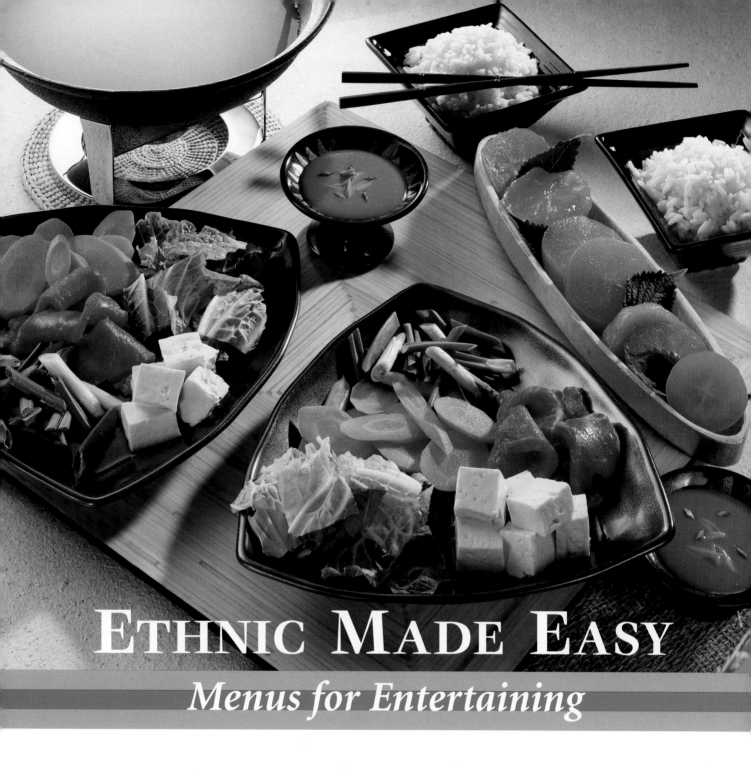

ETHNIC MADE EASY

Menus for Entertaining

Quick and Easy Cooking Series™

Cooking Club
of
America®

MINNETONKA, MINNESOTA

About the Author

Colleen Miner is a culinary consultant, television cooking personality, cooking teacher and cookbook author. Her lifelong passion for cooking started as a child when she spent all her spare time in the kitchen of her mother's restaurant. She lectures on food and entertaining throughout the United States, and is a professionally certified member of the International Association of Culinary Professionals as well as a member of Les Dame d'Escoffier Internationale. Colleen is the author of another Cooking Club of America title, *Easy Entertaining — Menus for Every Season.*

ETHNIC MADE EASY
Menus for Entertaining

Printed in 2005.

2 3 4 5 6 7 8 / 08 07 06 05
© 2003 Cooking Club of America
ISBN 1-58159-195-0

Cooking Club of America
12301 Whitewater Drive
Minnetonka, MN 55343
www.cookingclub.com

Tom Carpenter
Creative Director

Heather Koshiol
Managing Editor

Jennifer Guinea
Senior Book Development Coordinator

Jenya Prosmitsky
Book Design and Production

Gina Germ
Book Production

Laura Holle
Senior Book Development Assistant

Bill Lindner Photography
Commissioned Photography

Abby Wyckoff
Food Stylist

Kimberly Colburn
Pegi Lee
Susan Telleen
Assistant Food Stylists

Rhonda Watkins
Prop Stylist

Special thanks to: Terry Casey, Cindy Jurgensen, Nancy Lilleberg, Jason Lund, Nancy Maurer, Mary Jo Myers, Ruth Petran and Martha Zeimer.

TABLE OF CONTENTS

INTRODUCTION

There is no better way to entertain than with ethnic foods. Excitement, adventure, exploration, taste, romance … there are many good reasons to create food from another land when it's time to have a get-together or hold a celebration.

Unfortunately, ethnic food sometimes gets cumbersome to create. Excessive and difficult ingredient lists, coupled with what often becomes an inordinate amount of preparation time, can take all the fun out of ethnic cooking at home. That is, until *Ethnic Made Easy — Menus for Entertaining* found its way into your hands.

This book does away with long litanies of complex and hard-to-find ingredients. Instead, how does a simple list of only six or eight items long — and sometimes as few as two — sound? Time is the other factor that can scare the home chef away from new ideas. Who has all day to create a meal or party, especially when you want to have some energy left to enjoy yourself as well? That's why every recipe in this book takes 30 minutes or less (many of them much less!) to prepare, start to finish.

The 20 great menus to come — offering over a hundred recipes in all — will make short work of all your entertaining occasions. Find food native to Ireland, France, Scandinavia, Mexico, India, the Middle East, Indonesia, Italy, Morocco, Greece, Japan, Cuba, England, China, Russia and more. These ideas and instructions show you how to make real ethnic food without big hassles, huge expenses or immense amounts of time.

Ethnic Made Easy — Menus for Entertaining truly makes ethnic cooking quick and simple … but keeps all the taste and authenticity.

❖ **Hearty Irish Cottage Breakfast**

❖ **Très Élégant French Breakfast**

❖ **Scandinavian Brunch Smorgasbord**

❖ **Mexican Tequila Sunrise Brunch**

HEARTY IRISH COTTAGE BREAKFAST

There is nothing more quintessentially Irish than a hearty, homey breakfast. This is the classic morning meal that greets travelers staying at traditional Irish bed and breakfast establishments. It is some of the best food Ireland has to offer.

❖ **Steaming Hot Irish Porridge**

❖ **Honey Baked Fruits**

❖ **Ginger Scones**

❖ **Freshly Made Rhubarb Jam**

❖ **Mixed Grill with Tomatoes and Mushrooms**

for 6

Steaming Hot Irish Porridge

This is the simplest (and best) of breakfast fare. Porridge takes on excitement when topped with brown sugar, toasted nuts, baked fruit and, of course, cream.

6   **cups water**
1½   **teaspoons salt**
1½   **cups Irish-style rolled oats**

❖ In large saucepan, bring water and salt to a boil over high heat.

❖ Gradually add oats, stirring to avoid lumps. Cook over high heat, stirring constantly, until slightly thickened.

❖ Reduce heat; simmer about 20 minutes or until oatmeal is thick and soft.

Serves 6.

Preparation time: **30 minutes.**
Ready to serve: **30 minutes.**

Per serving: 150 calories, 2.5 g total fat (0.5 g saturated fat), 0 mg cholesterol, 585 mg sodium, 4 g fiber.

DO-AHEAD RECIPE IDEA
This oatmeal can be made the day before and reheated. Add milk to thin to desired consistency when reheated.

INGREDIENTS AND TIPS
Irish oatmeal is the gold standard for oatmeal. It is steel cut and looks more like barley than the rolled oats we are used to. It is found in the cereal aisle of most grocery stores.

Honey Baked Fruits

This fruit can be a breakfast in itself, but it also makes a great topping for the porridge (oatmeal).

1	**cup dried figs, quartered**
1	**cup dried apricots, quartered**
½	**cup dried cherries**
3	**bananas, peeled, cut into thick slices**
¼	**cup orange juice**
¼	**cup honey**

❖ Heat oven to 350°F.

❖ In microwave-safe bowl, combine figs, apricots and cherries. Add ¼ cup water; cover with plastic wrap. Microwave on High for 2 minutes to soften. Drain if necessary.

❖ Transfer softened fruit to shallow baking dish. Add bananas. In small bowl, combine orange juice and honey; blend well. Pour over fruit.

❖ Bake 20 minutes or until thoroughly heated. Serve warm.

Serves 6.

Preparation time: **5 minutes.**
Ready to serve: **25 minutes.**

Per serving: 275 calories, 1 g total fat (0 g saturated fat), 0 mg cholesterol, 5 mg sodium, 7 g fiber.

DO-AHEAD RECIPE IDEA
The fruit can be prepared and cooked earlier in the day, then reheated just before serving.

INGREDIENTS AND TIPS
Dried fruits have come a long way. New methods of drying and packaging leave the fruit moist, tender and sweet.

Ginger Scones

Crystallized ginger adds zing to these already delicious scones.

1¼	cups all-purpose flour
1½	teaspoons baking powder
2	tablespoons sugar
¼	teaspoon salt
¼	cup unsalted butter
⅓	cup milk
¼	cup finely chopped crystallized ginger

❖ Heat oven to 425°F.

❖ In medium bowl, combine flour, baking powder, sugar and salt; mix well. Cut in butter with a pastry blender until mixture resembles coarse crumbs. Add milk; stir until soft dough forms.

❖ Place dough on lightly floured surface. Add ginger; knead dough lightly until ginger is mixed in thoroughly.

❖ Divide dough in half. Pat each half into ½-inch-thick round. Cut each round into 8 wedges. Arrange wedges 1 inch apart on ungreased baking sheet.

❖ Bake 10 to 12 minutes or until golden brown. Serve warm.

Serves 6.

Preparation time: **15 minutes.**
Ready to serve: **30 minutes.**

Per serving: 210 calories, 8 g total fat (5 g saturated fat), 20 mg cholesterol, 250 mg sodium, 1 g fiber.

DO-AHEAD RECIPE IDEA
The dough can be made the day before, then covered with plastic wrap and refrigerated until ready to bake and serve. Scones are best served warm from the oven.

INGREDIENTS AND TIPS
Crystallized ginger is sugared preserved ginger. It might be available in the international aisle of your grocery store or in Asian markets.

Freshly Made Rhubarb Jam

Rhubarb is the perfect flavor accompaniment to the Ginger Scones (page 12). So, slather your scones with this thick, sweet-tart jam, and enjoy!

1   **(16-oz.) pkg. frozen cut rhubarb, thawed, drained and finely chopped**
2   **cups sugar**
1   **tablespoon lemon juice**

❖ In 8-cup microwave-safe bowl, combine rhubarb, sugar and lemon juice; stir to combine.

❖ Microwave on High about 8 minutes or until mixture becomes syrupy, stirring once halfway through cooking. Jam will continue to thicken as it cools. Serve with warm scones.

Serves 6.

Preparation time: **10 minutes.**
Ready to serve: **10 minutes.**

Per serving: 265 calories, 0 g total fat (0 g saturated fat), 0 mg cholesterol, 2 mg sodium, 1 g fiber.

DO-AHEAD RECIPE IDEA
This jam can be made ahead and refrigerated. It will keep in the refrigerator for a week.

INGREDIENTS AND TIPS
Rhubarb is technically a vegetable, but is so popular in pies, jams and compotes, that many people think of it as a fruit.

Mixed Grill with Tomatoes and Mushrooms

Ireland is famous for its hearty breakfasts, and this is the dish that makes that reputation well deserved.

12	**small pork sausages**
6	**lamb chops**
6	**slices cottage bacon**
8	**oz. large fresh white mushrooms**
6	**tomatoes, halved**
⅛	**teaspoon salt**
⅛	**teaspoon freshly ground pepper**

❖ Heat broiler.

❖ Place half of the sausages, lamb chops, bacon, mushrooms and tomatoes, cut side up, on broiler pan.

❖ Broil about 3 inches from heat about 10 minutes or until meat is thoroughly cooked, turning meat after 5 minutes and removing meat and vegetables from grill when thoroughly cooked; place on warm serving platter.

❖ Repeat broiling with remaining meat and vegetables.

Serves 6.

Preparation time: **10 minutes.**
Ready to serve: **20 minutes.**

Per serving: 350 calories, 20 g total fat (7 g saturated fat), 100 mg cholesterol, 735 mg sodium, 2 g fiber.

DO-AHEAD RECIPE IDEA
Prepare the mixed grill earlier and keep warm at 200°F until ready to serve.

INGREDIENTS AND TIPS
Cottage bacon is very similar to Canadian bacon, which can be used in this dish if cottage bacon is not available.

TRÈS ÉLÉGANT
FRENCH BREAKFAST

On most days the typical French breakfast is a simple Café au Lait and a crusty roll. But this is not your everyday breakfast. Here is a festive celebration meal featuring the "crème de la crème" of French morning cuisine.

❖ **Real French Toast**

❖ **Strawberries with Chantilly Cream**

❖ **Individual Brie Omelets**

❖ **Café au Lait**

❖ **Puff Pastry Spiral**

---

for 8

Real French Toast

In France, French toast is called pain perdu, *which translates into "lost bread." Why such an odd name? Because leftover stale bread is traditionally used! (Sounds sort of sad, but this really is a splendid breakfast "find.")*

2   **eggs**
⅓   **cup milk**
2   **tablespoons honey**
1   **tablespoon orange-flavored liqueur
    (optional)**
8   **(½-inch-thick) slices French bread**
1   **tablespoon butter**

❖ In shallow bowl, beat eggs until frothy. Stir in milk, honey and, if desired, liqueur.

❖ Dip bread slices into egg mixture, turning to coat. Let each slice absorb mixture, about 30 seconds.

❖ In large skillet, melt butter over medium heat until bubbly, about 30 seconds.

❖ Add bread slices; fry about 1 minute on each side or until golden.

❖ Serve French toast with syrup or *Strawberries with Chantilly Cream* (page 19).

Serves 8.

Preparation time: **5 minutes.**
Ready to serve: **10 minutes.**

Per serving: 195 calories, 8 g total fat (4 g saturated fat), 120 mg cholesterol, 220 mg sodium, 1 g fiber.

DO-AHEAD RECIPE IDEA
The day before, place the sliced bread in a coated baking dish and pour the egg-milk mixture over the bread. Cover and let the bread soak in the refrigerator overnight. Then bake the French toast at 350°F for 30 minutes.

INGREDIENTS AND TIPS
French bread is firm crusty bread that is made without preservatives. It makes a great sandwich one day and great French toast the next.

Strawberries with Chantilly Cream

Serve these delicious berries alone or as a topping for Real French Toast *(page 18)*.

2 cups ultra-pasteurized heavy whipping cream

¼ cup powdered sugar

2 tablespoons orange-flavored liqueur

1 quart fresh strawberries, sliced

❖ In large bowl, beat whipping cream, powdered sugar and liqueur with electric hand mixer until soft peaks form, about 3 minutes.

❖ Serve strawberries topped with whipped cream.

Serves 8.

Preparation time: **10 minutes.**
Ready to serve: **10 minutes.**

Per serving: 250 calories, 22 g total fat (14 g saturated fat), 80 mg cholesterol, 25 mg sodium, 2 g fiber.

DO-AHEAD RECIPE IDEA
The strawberries and cream can be prepared earlier in the day, covered and refrigerated until ready to serve.

INGREDIENTS AND TIPS
Ultra-pasteurized heavy whipping cream is useful for preparing ahead of time because it holds together for up to 3 hours in the refrigerator after whipping. It is available in the dairy case of most grocery stores.

Individual Brie Omelets

The French have a way with eggs. This very simple omelet can be made to order for each individual.

4	**eggs**
½	**teaspoon salt**
¼	**teaspoon freshly ground pepper, plus more to taste**
4	**teaspoons butter**
4	**oz. Brie, rind removed, cut into 8 slices**
⅛	**teaspoon salt**

❖ In medium bowl, beat eggs, ½ teaspoon salt and ¼ teaspoon pepper until thoroughly mixed. Set aside.

❖ In 8-inch nonstick omelet pan, melt ½ teaspoon of the butter over medium-high heat. Add 2 tablespoons egg mixture; immediately swirl egg

mixture around hot pan. Egg mixture will cook almost instantly, about 30 seconds.

- ❖ Place 1 cheese slice on one side of omelet; fold other side over cheese. Remove omelet from pan.

- ❖ Repeat with remaining butter and egg mixture to make 8 omelets. Season omelets to taste with salt and pepper.

Serves 8.

Preparation time: **5 minutes.**
Ready to serve: **15 minutes.**

Per serving: 100 calories, 8 g total fat (4.5 g saturated fat), 120 mg cholesterol, 295 mg sodium, 0 g fiber.

DO-AHEAD RECIPE IDEA
Beat the eggs ahead of time and remove the rind from the cheese.

INGREDIENTS AND TIPS
Brie is a creamy-mild cheese encased in an edible rind. The rind is removed in this recipe so the cheese will melt in the omelet.

Café au Lait

Adding hot milk to strong coffee makes an incredible difference in the taste of the end result.

4   cups milk
4   cups hot French roast coffee

❖ In large saucepan, heat milk until hot, but not boiling.

❖ For each drink, pour ½ cup steaming milk and ½ cup hot coffee at the same time into large cup.

Serves 8.

Preparation time: **10 minutes.**
Ready to serve: **10 minutes.**

Per serving: 60 calories, 2.5 g total fat (1.5 g saturated fat), 10 mg cholesterol, 65 mg sodium, 0 g fiber.

DO-AHEAD RECIPE IDEA
The coffee can be brewed ahead of time and kept warm in a thermal coffeepot.

INGREDIENTS AND TIPS
French roast coffee makes an ideal Café au Lait. The beans are roasted until very dark and this makes a stronger richer taste.

Puff Pastry Spiral

Keep the puff pastry quite cold while working with it, then put it into a hot oven immediately. These pastries are at their mouthwatering best served hot from the oven.

1   sheet frozen puff pastry, thawed
¼   cup sugar
1   teaspoon ground cinnamon

❖ Heat oven to 425°F. Line baking sheet with parchment paper.

❖ Unfold sheet of puff pastry. Gently roll with rolling pin to smooth out folds.

❖ In small bowl, mix sugar and cinnamon. Sprinkle sugar mixture evenly over pastry. Gently roll with rolling pin to press sugar mixture into pastry.

❖ Beginning with one long side, roll up pastry. With serrated knife using a sawing motion, cut roll into 16 (½-inch) slices. Place slices cut side down on lined baking sheet.

❖ Bake about 15 minutes or until golden brown. Remove from baking sheet; cool completely on wire rack.

Serves 8.

Preparation time: **15 minutes.**
Ready to serve: **30 minutes.**

Per serving: 230 calories, 14.5 g total fat (5 g saturated fat), 10 mg cholesterol, 75 mg sodium, 1 g fiber.

DO-AHEAD RECIPE IDEA
Assemble the rolls the day before and cut into slices.

INGREDIENTS AND TIPS
Puff pastry in France is called *mille-feuilles* which means "thousand leaves or layers." This may be an exaggeration, but the dough does contain numerous layers of dough and butter.

SCANDINAVIAN BRUNCH SMORGASBORD

The rugged sea-washed beauty of the Scandinavian countries is unsurpassed. The cuisine is fresh, simple and dominated by the sea that provides each country with work, play and sustenance. Smorgasbord buffet-style entertaining reflects the easy hospitality that is the hallmark of these countries.

❖ **Dilled Salmon Sandwich Platter**

❖ **Mustard Dill Sauce**

❖ **Swedish Pancakes**

❖ **Lingonberry Cream Sauce**

❖ **Scandinavian Breakfast Fruit Soup**

for 8

Dilled Salmon Sandwich Platter

Smörrebröd *means open-faced sandwich. It is a classic component of Scandinavian cuisine.*

½	**cup unsalted butter, softened**
12	**thin slices dark rye bread**
½	**lb. gravlax, thinly sliced, cut into triangles**
2	**large tomatoes, thinly sliced**
1	**cucumber, peeled, thinly sliced**
1	**red onion, thinly sliced**
1	**head Boston lettuce**

❖ Spread butter on rye bread slices.

❖ Arrange bread, gravlax, tomatoes, cucumber, onion and lettuce on serving platter. Serve with *Mustard Dill Sauce* (page 27).

Serves 8.

Preparation time: **25 minutes.**
Ready to serve: **25 minutes.**

Per serving: 235 calories, 14 g total fat (7.5 g saturated fat), 35 mg cholesterol, 430 mg sodium, 3 g fiber.

DO-AHEAD RECIPE IDEA
Slice the gravlax and vegetables early in the day.

INGREDIENTS AND TIPS
Gravlax is salmon cured in a salt and sugar mixture. It is served sliced paper-thin.

Mustard Dill Sauce

Dill is one of the dominant herbs in Scandinavian cuisine. Combined with Dijon mustard here, it creates a lovely sauce.

½ **cup Dijon mustard**
¼ **cup chopped fresh dill**

❖ In small bowl, combine mustard and dill; blend well. Serve with *Dilled Salmon Sandwich Platter* (page 26).

Serves 8.

Preparation time: **5 minutes.**
Ready to serve: **5 minutes.**

Per serving: 10 calories, 0.5 g total fat (0 g saturated fat), 0 mg cholesterol, 195 mg sodium, 0.5 g fiber.

DO-AHEAD RECIPE IDEA
Make the sauce the day before and refrigerate until ready to serve.

INGREDIENTS AND TIPS
If fresh dill is not available, substitute a tablespoon of dried dill.

Swedish Pancakes

Make these delicate pancakes thinner than traditional American pancakes and thicker than a French crêpe. Swedish Pancakes *are definitely in a class all their own.*

½	**cup all-purpose flour**
1	**tablespoon sugar**
¼	**teaspoon salt**
1	**cup milk**
½	**cup half-and-half or whipping cream**
3	**eggs**
2	**tablespoons butter, melted**

❖ In blender, combine flour, sugar, salt, milk, half-and-half and eggs; cover and blend until smooth.

❖ Heat griddle over medium-high heat until hot; brush with melted butter. For each pancake, drop 1 tablespoon batter onto griddle; cook about 2 minutes or until edges begin to brown. Turn; cook about 1 minute. Serve pancakes immediately with *Lingonberry Cream Sauce* (below), or stack and freeze.

Serves 8.

Preparation time: **5 minutes.**
Ready to serve: **25 minutes.**

Per serving: 145 calories, 10 g total fat (5.5 g saturated fat), 105 mg cholesterol, 135 mg sodium, 0 g fiber.

DO-AHEAD RECIPE IDEA

Make the batter the day before and refrigerate. The pancakes can be prepared earlier in the day, placed on a baking sheet, covered with foil and reheated at 200°F for about 10 minutes or until warm.

INGREDIENTS AND TIPS

A cast-iron plett pan with 3-inch circular indentations is perfect for making perfect pancakes.

Lingonberry Cream Sauce

This cream sauce makes the ideal topping for pancakes, ice cream and cakes.

1	**egg**
3	**tablespoons sugar**
2	**tablespoons cornstarch**
3	**cups half-and-half**
½	**cup lingonberry jam**
2	**teaspoons vanilla**

❖ In heavy saucepan, beat egg, sugar, cornstarch and half-and-half until well blended. Cook over low heat, stirring constantly, until mixture comes to a simmer. Simmer about 2 minutes or until slightly thickened, stirring constantly. Remove from heat. Stir in lingonberry jam and vanilla.

Serves 8.

Preparation time: **5 minutes.**
Ready to serve: **10 minutes.**

Per serving: 205 calories, 10 g total fat (6.5 g saturated fat), 60 mg cholesterol, 55 mg sodium, 0 g fiber.

DO-AHEAD RECIPE IDEA

Make the sauce the day before and refrigerate. Serve chilled or warm.

INGREDIENTS AND TIPS

The lingonberry is a member of the cranberry family and grows wild in the mountains of Scandinavia.

Scandinavian Breakfast Fruit Soup

This old-fashioned fruit soup is a standard in every Scandinavian country. The modern microwave helps make it in a jiffy ... and keep it full of taste.

6	**cups apple juice**
2	**(7-oz.) pkg. mixed dried fruit, coarsely chopped**
2	**cups frozen pitted cherries, thawed**
½	**cup sugar**
¼	**cup quick-cooking tapioca**
1	**tablespoon grated orange peel**
1	**cinnamon stick**
2	**cups whipping cream or half-and-half**

❖ In 8-cup microwave-safe bowl, combine apple juice, dried fruit, cherries, sugar, tapioca, orange peel and cinnamon stick.

❖ Microwave on High 15 to 20 minutes or until mixture boils and thickens. Remove cinnamon stick. Serve warm or cold with cream.

Serves 8.

Preparation time: **5 minutes.**
Ready to serve: **25 minutes.**

Per serving: 485 calories, 19 g total fat (11.5 g saturated fat), 65 mg cholesterol, 35 mg sodium, 5 g fiber.

DO-AHEAD RECIPE IDEA
Make this soup the day before and refrigerate, then served chilled. You can also reheat it to serve warm.

INGREDIENTS AND TIPS
Quick-cooking tapioca is a good thickening agent for pies as well as this soup.

MEXICAN TEQUILA SUNRISE BRUNCH

Mexican cuisine offers a kaleidoscope of bold flavors, varied textures and beautiful colors ... quite a wake-up call! Bring a hearty appetite for this robust ranch-style meal, and let it get your day off to a great start.

❖ **Huevos Rancheros**

❖ **Guacamole**

❖ **Tequila Sunrise**

❖ **Salsa Fresca**

❖ **Mexican Black Beans**

❖ **Sweet Banana Quesadillas**

for 8

Huevos Rancheros

Serve these "ranch-style" fried eggs on corn tortillas. What also makes them special are the toppings. So heap on the onions, cilantro, cheese, guacamole and black beans and enjoy!

4	**tablespoons butter**
16	**eggs**
16	**(6-inch) corn tortillas**
3	**white onions, chopped**
2	**cups chopped fresh cilantro**
4	**oz. queso fresco, crumbled**

❖ In large skillet, melt 2 tablespoons of the butter over medium-high heat. Add 8 eggs; fry until sunny-side up or to desired doneness. Remove eggs from skillet; place on large plate. Repeat with remaining eggs, adding additional butter if needed.

❖ Meanwhile, place tortillas in resealable plastic bag; seal, leaving small air vent. Microwave on High 1 minute. Remove from microwave. Wrap plastic bag with tortillas in clean towel to keep warm until ready to serve.

❖ For each serving, place 2 warm tortillas, overlapping, on dinner plate. Top with 2 fried eggs. Sprinkle with onions, cilantro and queso fresco to taste.

Serves 8.

Preparation time: **10 minutes.**
Ready to serve: **20 minutes.**

Per serving: 350 calories, 18 g total fat (7.5 g saturated fat), 445 mg cholesterol, 265 mg sodium, 3.5 g fiber.

DO-AHEAD RECIPE IDEA
Prepare the onions, cilantro and queso fresco earlier in the day. Cover and refrigerate until ready to use.

INGREDIENTS AND TIPS
Queso fresco is a fresh goat cheese. It is dry, crumbly and salty. If it is not available, feta cheese makes a good substitute.

White onions are preferred in Mexican cooking. They are sharper and not as sweet as yellow onions, and are readily available in all markets.

Guacamole

This combination of salsa and avocado is a traditional type of Guacamole *you might find in Mexico.*

2 cups salsa
3 avocados, pitted, peeled and mashed

❖ In medium bowl, combine salsa and mashed avocados; mix well. Cover; refrigerate until ready to serve.

Serves 8.

Preparation time: **5 minutes.**
Ready to serve: **5 minutes.**

Per serving: 120 calories, 10 g total fat (1.5 g saturated fat), 0 mg cholesterol, 175 mg sodium, 5 g fiber.

DO-AHEAD RECIPE IDEA
You can make this Guacamole earlier in the day.

INGREDIENTS AND TIPS
Any traditional tomato salsa will taste good in this sauce, so choose one that is to your liking. You may want to try your hand at making your own salsa using *Salsa Fresca* (page 38).

Tequila Sunrise

This drink is delicious and makes a beautiful presentation with or without the tequila.

1	**quart fresh orange juice**
½	**cup (4 oz.) tequila (optional)**
½	**cup grenadine**

❖ For each drink, pour about ½ cup orange juice over ice cubes in glass. Add tequila, if desired.

❖ Pour about 1 tablespoon grenadine carefully over back of spoon into glass to create streaks, like the rosy rays of sunrise.

Serves 8.

Preparation time: **5 minutes.**
Ready to serve: **5 minutes.**

Per serving: 130 calories, 0 g total fat (0 g saturated fat), 0 mg cholesterol, 0 mg sodium, 0 g fiber.

DO-AHEAD RECIPE IDEA
To make a really special drink, the orange juice can be fresh squeezed the day before.

INGREDIENTS AND TIPS
Grenadine is syrup made from the seed of pomegranates. It has a sweet fruity taste and a wonderful red color. It is available in liquor stores or the beverage aisle of most groceries.

Salsa Fresca

There are many good salsas on the market, but this fresca *(fresh) salsa is in a class of its own.*

2	**large tomatoes, seeded, finely diced**
½	**white onion, finely chopped**
½	**cup chopped fresh cilantro**
2	**jalapeño chiles, seeded, minced**
1	**garlic clove, minced**
2	**tablespoons lime juice**
¼	**teaspoon salt**

❖ In medium bowl, combine tomatoes, onion, cilantro, chiles, garlic, lime juice and salt; mix well.

Serves 8.

Preparation time: **20 minutes.**
Ready to serve: **20 minutes.**

Per serving: 25 calories, 0 g total fat (0 g saturated fat), 0 mg cholesterol, 105 mg sodium, 0 g fiber.

DO-AHEAD RECIPE IDEA
Make this salsa earlier in the day.

INGREDIENTS AND TIPS
Jalapeño chiles are hot green chiles. The smaller the jalapeño, the hotter it is. Much of the heat is located in the seeds, so seeding leaves the flavor and removes some of the heat.

Mexican Black Beans

In Mexico, a day without black beans is like a day without sunshine. Black beans offer a great earthy flavor, are delicious, and also serve as a great source of protein.

2 tablespoons olive oil
1 medium onion, diced
2 (15-oz.) cans black beans, undrained
½ cup chopped fresh cilantro
1 tablespoon ground cumin
⅛ teaspoon salt
⅛ teaspoon freshly ground pepper

❖ In large skillet, heat oil over medium heat until hot. Add onion; cook and stir 2 minutes or until soft.

❖ Add beans, cilantro and cumin; mix well. Reduce heat; simmer 15 minutes, stirring occasionally. Season with salt and pepper.

Serves 8.

Preparation time: **5 minutes.**
Ready to serve: **25 minutes.**

Per serving: 140 calories, 4 g total fat (0.5 g saturated fat), 0 mg cholesterol, 175 mg sodium, 5.5 g fiber.

DO-AHEAD RECIPE IDEA
Prepare these beans the day before and heat thoroughly before serving.

INGREDIENTS AND TIPS
Black beans are also called turtle beans. With their earthy flavor, they are a staple ingredient in Latin American cuisine.

Sweet Banana Quesadillas

These quesadillas *(grilled tortilla sandwiches) are a surprisingly sweet treat at a brunch.*

- **1   (8-oz.) pkg. cream cheese, softened**
- **8   (6-inch) flour tortillas**
- **4   bananas, peeled, sliced**
- **½   cup chopped honey-roasted peanuts**
- **2   tablespoons vegetable oil**
- **1   cup caramel sauce or ice cream topping, heated**

❖ Heat grill.

❖ Spread cream cheese evenly on tortillas. Arrange banana slices in single layer on half of each tortilla. Sprinkle each with peanuts.

❖ Fold untopped side of each tortilla over bananas. Brush each with oil.

❖ Place tortillas on gas grill over medium heat, on charcoal grill about 4 inches from medium coals, or in large skillet over medium-high heat. Cook about 3 minutes or until crisp and golden, turning once. Repeat with remaining tortillas. If using skillet, repeat with remaining folded tortillas.

❖ Cut each tortilla into wedges. Serve with warm caramel sauce.

Serves 8.

Preparation time: **15 minutes.**
Ready to serve: **20 minutes.**

Per serving: 480 calories, 20 g total fat (8 g saturated fat), 30 mg cholesterol, 500 mg sodium, 3.5 g fiber.

DO-AHEAD RECIPE IDEA
Assemble the quesadillas earlier in the day and cook just before serving.

INGREDIENTS AND TIPS
Flour tortillas are unleavened flat bread made with flour, lard and water. Heating before serving enhances the flavor.

LUNCHEONS

BOMBAY INDIAN VEGETARIAN LUNCHEON

Whether from the north, south, east or west of India, the country's cuisine is united by its use of abundant spices and vegetables. This vegetarian luncheon presents that classic Indian combination in a meal that will appeal to all.

❖ **Chickpea Curry**

❖ **Basmati Rice with Currants and Almonds**

❖ **Mango Chutney with Pappadams**

❖ **Garam Masala**

❖ **Mango Lassi**

---

for 4

Chickpea Curry

Since India has a large vegetarian population, the country is famous for its fabulous vegetarian dishes. This is one of them.

2	tablespoons vegetable oil
1	medium onion, diced
2	jalapeño chiles, seeded, minced
1	tablespoon minced fresh ginger
1	(15-oz.) can chickpeas, drained
1	(14.5-oz.) can diced tomatoes, undrained
2½	teaspoons garam masala
½	cup chopped fresh cilantro

❖ In large skillet, heat oil over medium heat until hot. Add onion, chiles and ginger; cook about 4 minutes or until onion is lightly browned, stirring frequently.

❖ Add chickpeas, tomatoes and garam masala; cook about 4 minutes or until thoroughly heated. Sprinkle with cilantro.

Serves 4.

Preparation time: **10 minutes.**
Ready to serve: **20 minutes.**

Per serving: 160 calories, 2 g total fat (0 g saturated fat), 0 mg cholesterol, 355 mg sodium, 6 g fiber.

DO-AHEAD RECIPE IDEA
Make this recipe the day before, then reheat.

INGREDIENTS AND TIPS
Garam masala is an Indian spice blend. There are many variations since each household has its own recipe. A standardized version is available in spice shops. If you cannot find it, make your own (page 50) or substitute a commercial curry powder.

Basmati Rice with Currants and Almonds

Rice with fruits, nuts and seasonings is called a puluo *in India. Dried currants and almonds give this rice a slightly sweet and nutty flavor, making it a perfect accompaniment for the hot curry.*

2	**tablespoons ghee or butter**
1	**cup basmati rice**
¼	**cup dried currants**
¼	**cup slivered almonds**
2	**cups vegetable broth**

❖ In large skillet, melt ghee over medium heat. Add rice, currants and almonds; cook and stir about 1 minute or until rice is coated.

❖ Add vegetable broth; bring to a boil. Reduce heat to low; cover and cook 20 minutes or until rice is tender and liquid is absorbed.

Serves 4.

Preparation time: **5 minutes.**
Ready to serve: **25 minutes.**

Per serving: 325 calories, 11.5 g total fat (4.5 g saturated fat), 15 mg cholesterol, 495 mg sodium, 2 g fiber.

DO-AHEAD RECIPE IDEA
Make this rice earlier in the day and reheat.

INGREDIENTS AND TIPS
Basmati rice is the fragrant, quick-cooking rice used in Indian cuisine.

Ghee is clarified butter, which means that all water, milk solids and other impurities are removed, leaving pure butter fat.

Mango Chutney with Pappadams

Chutney is a cooked mixture of fruit, vinegar, sugar and spices. Mangoes are plentiful in India and are a classic fruit for chutney.

8   pappadam wafers
1   (12-oz.) jar mango chutney
1   (8-oz.) pkg. cream cheese

❖ Place 2 pappadam wafers on microwave-safe plate. Microwave on High about 2 minutes or until completely puffed. Repeat with remaining wafers.

❖ Place cream cheese on serving platter. Pour chutney over top. Serve with pappadam wafers.

Serves 4.

Preparation time: **5 minutes.**
Ready to serve: **5 minutes.**

Per serving: 355 calories, 20 g total fat (12.5 g saturated fat), 60 mg cholesterol, 490 mg sodium, 3 g fiber.

DO-AHEAD RECIPE IDEA
You can make pappadams earlier in the day.

INGREDIENTS AND TIPS
Pappadams are 6-inch wafers made of lentil flour. They expand and puff up when deep-fried or microwaved. They are a great accompaniment for curries. Pappadams can be found in Indian markets. Crackers can be substituted.

Garam Masala

Here is a classic recipe for this wonderful spice mixture.

4   **tablespoons coriander seeds**
2   **tablespoons cumin seeds**
1   **tablespoon whole peppercorns**
2   **teaspoons cardamom pods**
1   **teaspoon whole cloves**
4   **cinnamon sticks**

❖ In heavy saucepan, roast each spice separately over medium heat, stirring to keep spice from burning. Spice will release its fragrance when done. Each spice will take a different amount of time to roast.

❖ Place all spices in spice grinder or food processor; grind until a powder forms.

Makes about ½ cup.

Preparation time: **15 minutes.**
Ready to serve: **15 minutes.**

Per serving: 5 calories, 0.5 g total fat (0 g saturated fat), 0 mg cholesterol, 0 mg sodium, 0.5 g fiber.

DO-AHEAD RECIPE IDEA
You can make this spice blend in advance.

INGREDIENTS AND TIPS
Store the garam masala in an airtight container in a cool dry place. The flavor will last for months.

Mango Lassi

Mango Lassi cools any of the heat generated by the chiles in an Indian meal. This beverage offers the richness of an ice cream shake, and serves as a refreshing dessert in this luncheon.

1½	**cups buttermilk or yogurt, chilled**
1	**cup mango pulp, chilled**
1	**cup cold water**
3	**tablespoons sugar**
2	**teaspoons lime juice**

❖ In blender, combine buttermilk, mango pulp, water, sugar and lime juice; cover and process until well blended and frothy.

❖ Pour mixture into pitcher. Serve immediately, or refrigerate until serving time.

Serves 4.

Preparation time: **5 minutes.**
Ready to serve: **5 minutes.**

Per serving: 120 calories, 1.5 g total fat (1 g saturated fat), 5 mg cholesterol, 65 mg sodium, 1 g fiber.

DO-AHEAD RECIPE IDEA
Combine all ingredients the day before and chill until ready to serve.

INGREDIENTS AND TIPS
Mango pulp is available in many ethnic markets. You can make your own by draining and puree-ing a can of mangoes.

THAI PICNIC

Although Thailand is but a small country in southeast Asia, its cuisine is becoming hugely popular. The intense flavors of tropical spices and sweet fruits combine in a graceful balance that is the essence of this ancient kingdom of Siam.

❖ **Thai Beef Salad**

❖ **Lime Dressing**

❖ **Velvety Chicken and Ginger Soup**

❖ **Thai Fruit and Coconut Cocktail**

for 8

Thai Beef Salad

Salads that combine hot meats and cool vegetables are a staple in Thai cuisine. This salad is a traditional dish in northeastern Thailand.

2 **lb. beef sirloin steak (½ inch thick)**
8 **cups sliced Napa cabbage**
1 **red onion, thinly sliced**
½ **cup chopped fresh cilantro**
¼ **cup chopped fresh Thai basil**
¼ **cup sesame seeds**
1 **recipe prepared *Lime Dressing* (page 57)**
½ **cup chopped peanuts**

❖ Heat grill.

❖ Place steak on gas grill over medium heat or on charcoal grill 4 to 6 inches from medium coals. Cook about 5 minutes on each side or until of desired doneness. Let steak stand 10 minutes before slicing.

❖ Meanwhile, in large salad bowl, combine cabbage, onion, cilantro, basil and sesame seeds; toss to combine.

❖ Cut steak across grain into thin slices. Top salad with steak slices. Pour Lime Dressing over salad. Sprinkle with peanuts.

Serves 8.

Preparation time: **10 minutes.**
Ready to serve: **25 minutes.**

Per serving: 215 calories, 10 g total fat (2 g saturated fat), 60 mg cholesterol, 125 mg sodium, 2 g fiber.

DO-AHEAD RECIPE IDEA
Assemble the salad earlier in the day. Add the beef and peanuts at the last minute.

INGREDIENTS AND TIPS
Thai basil has a sweet slightly anise flavor, but you can substitute domestic basil with good results.

Lime Dressing

This dressing complements Thai Beef Salad *(page 56), but is great on other salads as well.*

¼ **cup lime juice**
¼ **cup soy sauce**
1 **tablespoon brown sugar**
1 **tablespoon peanut oil**
1 **teaspoon sambal oelek or chili paste**

❖ In medium bowl, combine lime juice, soy sauce, brown sugar, oil and sambal oelek; stir gently to mix.

Serves 8.

Preparation time: **5 minutes.**
Ready to serve: **5 minutes.**

Per serving: 55 calories, 3.5 g total fat (0.5 g saturated fat), 0 mg cholesterol, 1050 mg sodium, 0 g fiber.

DO-AHEAD RECIPE IDEA
You can make this sauce the day before.

INGREDIENTS AND TIPS
Sambal oelek is a hot paste made from fresh chiles mashed and mixed with salt. Chili paste or crushed red pepper make acceptable substitutes.

Velvety Chicken and Ginger Soup

In Thailand this soup is made with fresh galangal root, which is very much like fresh ginger.

3	cups coconut milk
2	cups chicken broth
2	tablespoons minced fresh ginger
½	lb. boneless skinless chicken breast halves, cut into thin strips
2	tablespoons fish sauce
1	teaspoon garlic-chili sauce
1	cup chopped fresh cilantro

❖ In large saucepan, combine coconut milk, chicken broth and ginger. Bring to a boil over medium-high heat. Reduce heat; simmer 5 minutes, stirring occasionally.

❖ Add chicken, fish sauce and garlic-chili sauce; mix well. Simmer about 5 minutes or until chicken is thoroughly cooked and soup is thoroughly heated. Stir in cilantro.

Serves 8.

Preparation time: **10 minutes.**
Ready to serve: **20 minutes.**

Per serving: 225 calories, 20 g total fat (17 g saturated fat), 15 mg cholesterol, 465 mg sodium, 0 g fiber.

DO-AHEAD RECIPE IDEA
Make this soup the day before and serve warm or at room temperature.

INGREDIENTS AND TIPS
Fish sauce is a salty, pungent flavored sauce made from fermented small fish and shrimp. Its strong flavor diminishes when cooked with other ingredients. Find it in the international aisle of grocery stores, or in Asian markets.

Thai Fruit and Coconut Cocktail

These Asian fruits turn an ordinary fruit cocktail into an exotic treat.

1 **(15-oz.) can lychees, drained**
1 **(15-oz.) can mangoes, drained**
1 **(15-oz.) can loquats, drained**
½ **cup sweetened cream of coconut**
½ **cup coconut**

❖ In large decorative bowl, combine lychees, mangoes, loquats, cream of coconut and coconut; stir gently to combine.

Serves 8.

Preparation time: **5 minutes.**
Ready to serve: **5 minutes.**

Per serving: 125 calories, 5 g total fat (4.5 g saturated fat), 0 mg cholesterol, 15 mg sodium, 2 g fiber.

DO-AHEAD RECIPE IDEA
Combine the fruit the day before and chill until ready to serve. Toss with cream of coconut and coconut at the last minute.

INGREDIENTS AND TIPS
Cream of coconut is used in cocktails like piña coladas and is found in the beverage aisle of grocery stores or in liquor stores.

MIDDLE EASTERN SALAD LUNCHEON

*The once exotic treasures of the Middle East —
pomegranates, pistachios and pita bread — are
now available for us to enjoy in this luncheon
that conjures images of an oasis in the desert.*

❖ **Red Bell Pepper, Walnut and Pomegranate Dip**

❖ **Toasted Herbed Pita Bread**

❖ **Tabbouleh Salad with Feta and Vegetables**

❖ **Pistachio Cream Stuffed Apricots**

❖ **Middle Eastern Spiced Coffee**

for 6

Red Bell Pepper, Walnut and Pomegranate Dip

Prepared roasted red bell peppers make preparing this dip a snap. If they are not available, you can roast your own by placing bell peppers under the broiler until blackened, then peel and core.

1	**(12-oz.) jar roasted red bell peppers, drained**
½	**cup walnuts**
1	**garlic clove**
2	**tablespoons olive oil**
1	**teaspoon cumin seeds**
1	**teaspoon pomegranate syrup (optional)**

❖ In blender or food processor, combine roasted peppers, walnuts, garlic, oil, cumin seeds and syrup, if desired; process until smooth. Serve with *Toasted Herbed Pita Bread* (below).

Serves 6.

Preparation time: **5 minutes.**
Ready to serve: **5 minutes.**

Per serving: 110 calories, 10 g total fat (0 g saturated fat), 0 mg cholesterol, 120 mg sodium, 0 g fiber.

DO-AHEAD RECIPE IDEA
You can prepare this dish the day before.

INGREDIENTS AND TIPS
Pomegranate syrup is a thick dark syrup made from pomegranate juice. It is often used in combination with walnuts in Middle Eastern cooking.

Toasted Herbed Pita Bread

There are two types of pita bread — one with and one without a pocket. Pocket pita breads are great for sandwiches. Flat-bread pitas are great for dipping, but either would work here.

6	**pita breads**
2	**tablespoons olive oil**
3	**tablespoons za'atar (optional)**
2	**teaspoons salt**

❖ Heat oven to 400°F.

❖ Brush pita breads with oil. Sprinkle each with za'atar, if desired, and salt. Place on baking sheet.

❖ Bake 3 minutes or just until thoroughly heated. Cut each bread into wedges. Serve with *Red Bell Pepper, Walnut and Pomegranate Dip* (above).

Serves 6.

Preparation time: **5 minutes.**
Ready to serve: **10 minutes.**

Per serving: 175 calories, 6 g total fat (1 g saturated fat), 0 mg cholesterol, 1015 mg sodium, 1.5 g fiber.

DO-AHEAD RECIPE IDEA
Bread can be topped earlier in the day, but should be baked just before serving.

INGREDIENTS AND TIPS
Za'atar is a spice blend that is a mixture of sesame seeds, thyme, marjoram and sumac.

Tabbouleh Salad with Feta and Vegetables

A tabbouleh mix contains all the seasonings, so you can concentrate on preparing the vegetables.

1 (5.25-oz.) pkg. tabbouleh mix	⅓ cup pitted Kalamata olives
1½ cups hot water	⅓ cup feta cheese
1 cup sliced cucumber	2 tablespoons lemon juice
1 cup grape tomatoes	2 tablespoons olive oil
⅔ cup chopped fresh parsley	

❖ In large salad bowl, combine tabbouleh mix and hot water; stir to combine. Cool about 15 minutes.

❖ Add cucumber, tomatoes, parsley, olives, feta cheese, lemon juice and oil; toss gently to combine.

Serves 6.

Preparation time: **15 minutes.**
Ready to serve: **30 minutes.**

Per serving: 165 calories, 7 g total fat (2 g saturated fat), 5 mg cholesterol, 570 mg sodium, 5.5 g fiber.

DO-AHEAD RECIPE IDEA
You can make this salad the day before.

INGREDIENTS AND TIPS
Bulgur wheat is the main ingredient in tabbouleh. This wheat is hulled, then boiled, dried and cracked. It requires little or no cooking.

Pistachio Cream Stuffed Apricots

Mediterranean dried apricots are very moist and sweet. They are left whole, but because they are pitted they are perfect for stuffing.

18   **whole Mediterranean dried apricots**
1   **(8-oz.) pkg. cream cheese, softened**
½   **cup finely chopped, shelled pistachios**
3   **tablespoons sugar**
1   **teaspoon rose water**

❖ Place apricots in microwave-safe bowl. Add ¼ cup water; cover with plastic wrap.

❖ Microwave on High 1 minute to soften. Drain; cool apricots.

❖ While apricots are cooling, in medium bowl, combine cream cheese, ¼ cup of the pistachios, sugar and rose water; mix well.

❖ Open each apricot along seam left from pitting. Stuff each apricot with 1 tablespoon cream cheese mixture; press together. Arrange on serving platter. Sprinkle with remaining pistachios.

Serves 6.

Preparation time: **10 minutes.**
Ready to serve: **10 minutes.**

Per serving: 90 calories, 6 g total fat (3 g saturated fat), 15 mg cholesterol, 40 mg sodium, 0 g fiber.

DO-AHEAD RECIPE IDEA
The cream cheese mixture can be made the day before. Stuff the apricots just before serving.

INGREDIENTS AND TIPS
Rose water is the distilled essence extracted from roses. It is used to perfume sweets and drinks. You can find rose water in health food stores, herb stores and delicatessens.

Middle Eastern Spiced Coffee

Put away the large coffee mugs. This thick and spicy coffee is meant to be taken in small amounts only ... and sipped and savored slowly.

8	cardamom pods, smashed
2	cups cold water
½	cups coarse-ground dark-roast coffee beans

❖ In large saucepan, combine cardamom pods, water and ground coffee beans. Bring to a boil over medium-high heat.

❖ Reduce heat to low; simmer 20 minutes or until coffee is concentrated and strong.

❖ Pour coffee through fine strainer into cups.

Serves 6.

Preparation time: **5 minutes.**
Ready to serve: **25 minutes.**

Per serving: 0 calories, 0 g total fat (0 g saturated fat), 0 mg cholesterol, 0 mg sodium, 0 g fiber.

DO-AHEAD RECIPE IDEA
This coffee can be made ahead and strained, then reheated just before serving.

INGREDIENTS AND TIPS
Cardamom is a spice more often associated with pastries than beverages. In Asia and the Middle East, cardamom is considered to aid digestion after a meal.

ITALIAN LUNCHEON

In Italy, lunch is a time for the family to gather for lively conversation over a meal that includes the classic ingredients — garlic, olive oil and pasta. Enjoy the essence of Bella Italia with these savory and sweet dishes.

❖ **Bagna Cauda Garlic Dip**

❖ **Linguine with White Clam Sauce**

❖ **Spinach and Pine Nut Salad**

❖ **Pears, Honey and Gorgonzola**

for 4

Bagna Cauda Garlic Dip

This dip, whose name translates to "hot bath," is the Italian version of fondue. Dip vegetables into the hot flavored oil, and use the bread as an edible napkin to help catch the drips.

½ cup butter

¼ cup olive oil

3 garlic cloves, minced

1 (2-oz.) can anchovies, drained, chopped

4 cups assorted sliced vegetables (such as bell peppers, zucchini, artichokes, mushrooms and carrots)

1 loaf Italian bread, sliced

❖ In small saucepan, combine butter, oil, garlic and anchovies. Cook and stir over low heat until thoroughly heated.

❖ To keep warm at table, place in fondue-type pot over a low-heat source.

❖ Arrange sliced vegetables and bread on serving platter. Serve with toothpicks for dipping.

Serves 4.

Preparation time: **20 minutes**.
Ready to serve: **25 minutes**.

Per serving: 610 calories, 40 g total fat (17 g saturated fat), 70 mg cholesterol, 1075 mg sodium, 4.5 g fiber.

DO-AHEAD RECIPE IDEA
Prepare the vegetables the day before and refrigerate until ready to serve.

INGREDIENTS AND TIPS
Anchovies are small fish from the herring family that are cured and packed in oil.

Linguine with White Clam Sauce

Mild and sweet clams become pure culinary perfection when prepared in this simple pasta dish.

12	**oz. linguine**
3	**tablespoons butter**
2	**garlic cloves, minced**
½	**teaspoon crushed red pepper**
1	**(10-oz.) can whole clams, undrained**
1	**cup chopped fresh Italian parsley**
½	**cup white wine**

❖ Cook linguine according to package directions. Drain.

❖ Meanwhile, in large saucepan, melt butter over medium heat. Add garlic and crushed red pepper; sauté 1 minute.

❖ Reduce heat. Add clams, ½ cup of the parsley and wine; cook about 3 minutes or until all ingredients are thoroughly heated.

❖ Add cooked linguine; toss to coat. Place on serving platter. Sprinkle with remaining ½ cup parsley.

Serves 4.

Preparation time: **10 minutes.**
Ready to serve: **20 minutes.**

Per serving: 475 calories, 11 g total fat (5.5 g saturated fat), 45 mg cholesterol, 505 mg sodium, 3.5 g fiber.

DO-AHEAD RECIPE IDEA
Make the linguine the day before, rinse with cold water and store in the refrigerator. To reheat linguine, place in a colander over boiling water and steam it.

INGREDIENTS AND TIPS
Italian parsley is also called flat-leaf parsley and is stronger tasting than curly parsley. If it is not available, curly parsley can be substituted.

Spinach and Pine Nut Salad

This is a classic Italian combination of ingredients. They are often cooked together, but here they combine to create a fresh and delicious salad.

6	cups fresh spinach
⅓	cup pine nuts, toasted
⅓	cup golden raisins
⅓	cup olive oil
2	tablespoons lemon juice
2	tablespoons honey

❖ In large salad bowl, combine spinach, pine nuts and raisins.

❖ In small bowl, combine oil, lemon juice and honey; whisk until well blended. Pour dressing over salad; toss to combine.

Serves 4.

Preparation time: **15 minutes.**
Ready to serve: **15 minutes.**

Per serving: 305 calories, 24 g total fat (3.5 g saturated fat), 0 mg cholesterol, 75 mg sodium, 4 g fiber.

DO-AHEAD RECIPE IDEA
Assemble this salad and dressing earlier in the day and toss all ingredients together at the last minute.

INGREDIENTS AND TIPS
Pine nuts, which are called *pignoli* in Italy, are a small soft nut. They should be frozen to keep from going rancid and to retain flavor.

Pears, Honey and Gorgonzola

Drizzle fruit and cheese with honey to create a light and classic Italian dessert.

2 ripe Bosc pears, halved, cored
4 oz. Gorgonzola cheese
½ cup honey

❖ Place each pear half on individual dessert plate.

❖ Top each with cheese. Drizzle with honey.

Serves 4.

Preparation time: **10 minutes.**
Ready to serve: **10 minutes.**

Per serving: 275 calories, 8.5 g total fat (5.5 g saturated fat), 20 mg cholesterol, 395 mg sodium, 2 g fiber.

DO-AHEAD RECIPE IDEA
Don't wait until the last minute to buy pears. They are seldom ripe in the stores and may take as long as 5 days to ripen.

INGREDIENTS AND TIPS
Gorgonzola is an Italian blue cheese. Serve at room temperature for maximum flavor.

INDONESIAN RIJSTTAFEL

The Dutch colonists introduced the rijsttafel *or "rice table feast" to Indonesia as a way to enjoy the vast variety of Indonesian dishes all at once. The feast's centerpiece is a platter of mounded golden rice. The platter is then surrounded by as many as 40 small dishes of meat, vegetables and condiments. It was definitely a meal that required a staff of servants! This menu gives a hint of the feast without all the work.*

❖ **Gado Gado Vegetable Platter**

❖ **Indonesian Peanut Dipping Sauce**

❖ **Hot Curried Shrimp**

❖ **Golden Turmeric Rice**

❖ **Katsup Manis**

for 6

Gado Gado Vegetable Platter

This platter always features potatoes and hard-cooked eggs, but feel free to add your own favorite vegetables!

6	small new potatoes
2	cups trimmed fresh green beans
2	medium carrots, sliced
8	oz. fresh bean sprouts
1	medium cucumber, peeled, sliced
1	medium green bell pepper, seeded, cut into strips
3	hard-cooked eggs, peeled, quartered

❖ In microwave-safe bowl, microwave potatoes on High about 5 minutes or until tender. Drain; cut potatoes into quarters. Meanwhile, in large saucepan of boiling water, blanch green beans and carrots for about 1 minute. Drain; rinse with cold water. Arrange all vegetables and eggs on serving platter. Serve with *Indonesian Peanut Dipping Sauce* (below).

Serves 6.

Preparation time: **25 minutes.**
Ready to serve: **25 minutes.**

Per serving: 115 calories, 3 g total fat (1 g saturated fat), 105 mg cholesterol, 50 mg sodium, 3.5 g fiber.

DO-AHEAD RECIPE IDEA
All the vegetables can be prepared the day before, covered and refrigerated.

INGREDIENTS AND TIPS
Bean sprouts are the growth of the mung bean. They are available in the produce section of your grocery store.

Indonesian Peanut Dipping Sauce

This is the traditional dip for the Gado Gado Vegetable Platter *(above).*

1	tablespoon vegetable oil
1	medium onion, minced
1	cup coconut milk
½	cup peanut butter
½	cup water
1	tablespoon fish sauce
1	tablespoon prepared *Katsup Manis* (page 88)
1	teaspoon crushed red pepper

❖ In medium saucepan, heat oil over medium heat until hot. Add onion; cook about 3 minutes or until softened, stirring occasionally. Add coconut milk, peanut butter, water, fish sauce, Katsup Manis and crushed red pepper; mix well. Cook over medium heat until thoroughly heated, stirring frequently.

Serves 6.

Preparation time: **5 minutes.**
Ready to serve: **10 minutes.**

Per serving: 240 calories, 22 g total fat (10 g saturated fat), 0 mg cholesterol, 310 mg sodium, 2 g fiber.

DO-AHEAD RECIPE IDEA
This sauce can be made the day before.

INGREDIENTS AND TIPS
Peanut butter is a staple ingredient in East Asian cooking and sauces. In Asia, it would be freshly ground from peanuts, but commercial peanut butter is a good and easy substitute.

Hot Curried Shrimp

Indonesian cooking has been influenced greatly by its trading neighbors. This shrimp curry is an émigré from Indian cuisine. If the shrimp have too much heat, reduce the amount of red pepper to suit your palate.

2   **tablespoons peanut oil**
2   **medium onions, minced**
1   **garlic clove, minced**
1   **tablespoon minced fresh ginger**
1   **(28-oz.) can diced tomatoes, undrained**
½   **cup water**
1   **tablespoon curry powder**
1   **tablespoon crushed red pepper**
1   **lb. shelled, deveined uncooked medium shrimp**

❖ In large skillet, heat oil over medium-high heat until hot. Add onions, garlic and ginger; cook and stir until golden brown.

❖ Add tomatoes, water, curry powder and crushed red pepper; mix well. Reduce heat; cover and simmer 10 minutes or until mixture is slightly thickened.

❖ Add shrimp; simmer an additional 3 minutes or until shrimp turn pink. Serve with *Golden Turmeric Rice* (page 87).

Serves 6.

Preparation time: **15 minutes.**
Ready to serve: **30 minutes.**

Per serving: 160 calories, 6 g total fat (1 g saturated fat), 140 mg cholesterol, 385 mg sodium, 2.5 g fiber.

DO-AHEAD RECIPE IDEA
Make the sauce ahead, then add the shrimp and cook just before serving.

INGREDIENTS AND TIPS
Curry powder is a spice blend developed by the English to re-create the flavors of the stews they grew to love in India.

Golden Turmeric Rice

This beautiful golden rice serves as the centerpiece of the rice table. For a large party, shape the rice into a high cone on a serving platter.

2	**cups water**
2	**cups coconut milk**
2	**cups jasmine rice**
1	**teaspoon salt**
½	**teaspoon turmeric**
½	**teaspoon coriander**

❖ In large saucepan, bring water and coconut milk to a boil over medium-high heat.

❖ Stir in rice, salt, turmeric and coriander. Reduce heat to low; cover and cook 20 minutes or until rice is tender.

Serves 6.

Preparation time: **25 minutes.**
Ready to serve: **25 minutes.**

Per serving: 405 calories, 17.5 g total fat (15 g saturated fat), 0 mg cholesterol, 400 mg sodium, 1 g fiber.

DO-AHEAD RECIPE IDEA
Make this rice the day before and reheat just before serving.

INGREDIENTS AND TIPS
Jasmine rice is a variety of long-grain rice, distinctive for its soft texture and lovely light fragrance. Any long-grain rice can be substituted.

Katsup Manis

This is a very good facsimile of commercial Indonesian soy sauce or Katsup Manis. *It is sometimes called sweet soy sauce.*

½   **cup packed dark brown sugar**
½   **cup granulated sugar**
1   **cup soy sauce**
1   **teaspoon minced fresh ginger**
2   **pods star anise**

❖ In medium saucepan, combine brown sugar, granulated sugar, soy sauce, ginger and star anise; mix well. Bring to a boil over medium-high heat, stirring constantly.

❖ Reduce heat; simmer about 10 minutes or until sugars are dissolved and mixture has thickened, stirring frequently. Remove from heat; cool completely.

❖ Strain mixture to remove ginger and star anise. Place mixture in jar; cover and refrigerate until ready to use. Mixture will keep for about 3 months.

Serves 6.

Preparation time: **10 minutes.**
Ready to serve: **10 minutes.**

Per serving: 15 calories, 0 g total fat (0 g saturated fat), 0 mg cholesterol, 230 mg sodium, 0 g fiber.

DO-AHEAD RECIPE IDEA
This sauce can be made the day before.

INGREDIENTS AND TIPS
Star anise is a star-shaped dark brown pod that grows on a small evergreen tree. It has a pronounced licorice flavor.

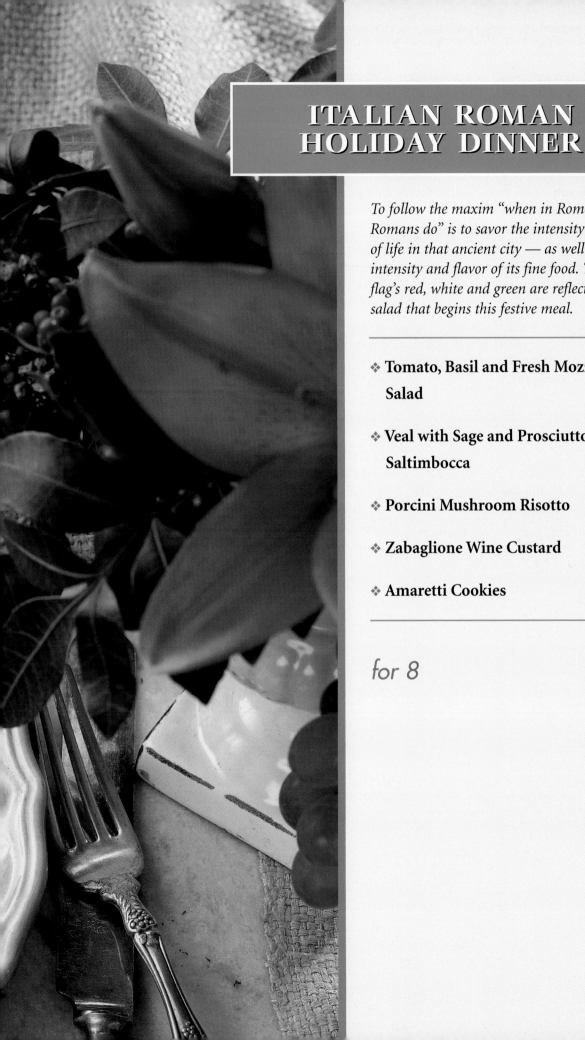

ITALIAN ROMAN HOLIDAY DINNER

To follow the maxim "when in Rome, do as the Romans do" is to savor the intensity and flavor of life in that ancient city — as well as the intensity and flavor of its fine food. The Italian flag's red, white and green are reflected in the salad that begins this festive meal.

❖ **Tomato, Basil and Fresh Mozzarella Salad**

❖ **Veal with Sage and Prosciutto Saltimbocca**

❖ **Porcini Mushroom Risotto**

❖ **Zabaglione Wine Custard**

❖ **Amaretti Cookies**

for 8

Tomato, Basil and Fresh Mozzarella Salad

This is a splendid dish for entertaining. It looks like you spent a great deal of time fussing when you really only invested a few minutes!

1	teaspoon salt
4	large tomatoes, sliced
4	balls fresh mozzarella, sliced (about 8 oz.)
1	cup shredded fresh basil
½	cup olive oil

❖ Sprinkle salt over tomato slices.

❖ On large serving platter, alternate tomato slices and cheese slices in circular pattern.

❖ Sprinkle basil on top. Drizzle with oil.

Serves 8.

Preparation time: **15 minutes.**
Ready to serve: **15 minutes.**

Per serving: 220 calories, 21 g total fat (6 g saturated fat), 20 mg cholesterol, 440 mg sodium, 1 g fiber.

DO-AHEAD RECIPE IDEA
You can assemble this salad earlier in the day.

INGREDIENTS AND TIPS
Fresh mozzarella consists of medium or small balls of uncured mozzarella that are stored in water or marinated in herbed oil. This cheese is soft and quite bland ... perfect to add subtle spicing to.

Veal with Sage and Prosciutto Saltimbocca

"Jump-in-the-mouth" — that's the translation of saltimbocca. *You'll discover why when you taste these wonderfully delicious veal packets.*

16	**veal scaloppine slices (about 2 lb.)**
16	**fresh sage leaves**
16	**slices prosciutto (about 4 oz.)**
16	**slices fontina cheese (about 6 oz.)**
4	**tablespoons butter**
1	**cup dry Marsala wine**

❖ On each veal scaloppine slice, place 1 sage leaf, 1 prosciutto slice and 1 cheese slice. Fold veal slices in half to form packets; secure with toothpicks.

❖ In large skillet, heat 2 tablespoons of the butter over medium-high heat until bubbly. Add half of the packets; cook about 3 minutes on each side or until brown.

❖ Remove veal from skillet; place on warm serving platter and cover with aluminum foil to keep warm. Repeat with remaining veal packets, adding additional butter to skillet if necessary.

❖ Add wine to skillet, stirring to deglaze; cook and stir about 2 minutes or until slightly thickened. Pour sauce over veal.

Serves 8.

Preparation time: **10 minutes.**
Ready to serve: **25 minutes.**

Per serving: 285 calories, 18 g total fat (10 g saturated fat), 115 mg cholesterol, 345 mg sodium, 0 g fiber.

DO-AHEAD RECIPE IDEA
You can assemble the veal packets earlier in the day.

INGREDIENTS AND TIPS
Prosciutto is an Italian ham that has been cured by salting and drying in the air. Any thin-sliced ham can be substituted.

Porcini Mushroom Risotto

Fresh porcini mushrooms are seldom found outside of Italy because they are so delicate. The dried porcini in this risotto carry a strong and woodsy flavor.

2	cups chicken broth
1	oz. dried porcini mushrooms
2	tablespoons olive oil
¼	cup chopped onion
1	cup Arborio or short-grain rice
¼	cup freshly grated Parmesan cheese

❖ In medium saucepan, bring chicken broth and mushrooms to a simmer over low heat. Cook about 5 minutes or until mushrooms are soft.

❖ Meanwhile, in large skillet, heat oil over medium heat until hot. Add onion; cook 2 minutes. Add rice; cook an additional 2 minutes, stirring to coat.

❖ Add warm broth and mushrooms to rice mixture, stirring to combine. Reduce heat to low; cover and cook about 25 minutes or until broth is absorbed and rice is tender. Remove from heat. Stir in cheese.

Serves 8.

Preparation time: **5 minutes.**
Ready to serve: **30 minutes.**

Per serving: 130 calories, 4 g total fat (0.5 g saturated fat), 0 mg cholesterol, 260 mg sodium, 0.5 g fiber.

DO-AHEAD RECIPE IDEA
Cook the rice ahead of time and heat thoroughly just before serving.

INGREDIENTS AND TIPS
Arborio rice is short-grain rice used to make risotto because it absorbs a lot of liquid and becomes creamy, but stays firm.

Zabaglione Wine Custard

Make this soft, frothy and delicious custard in a double boiler. If you don't have a double boiler, use a stainless steel bowl that fits snugly into a saucepan.

8	**egg yolks**
2	**whole eggs**
½	**cup superfine sugar**
½	**cup Marsala wine**

❖ In top half of double boiler, combine egg yolks, eggs, sugar and wine; whisk to combine.

❖ Place over simmering water in bottom half of double boiler. Cook about 5 minutes or until custard is thick enough to mound slightly and reaches 160°F, whisking constantly.

❖ Immediately pour custard into wine glasses. Serve with *Amaretti Cookies* (below).

Serves 8.

Preparation time: **5 minutes.**
Ready to serve: **10 minutes.**

Per serving: 135 calories, 6.5 g total fat (2 g saturated fat), 265 mg cholesterol, 25 mg sodium, 0 g fiber.

DO-AHEAD RECIPE IDEA
The eggs can be separated the day before. The yolks should be refrigerated in a tightly covered container. The whites can be frozen for use at another time.

INGREDIENTS AND TIPS
Marsala is a sweet fortified wine.

Amaretti Cookies

These delicate little cookies are really the Italian version of macaroons. They are the perfect crunchy accompaniment to the frothy Zabaglione Wine Custard *(above).*

1	**cup blanched whole almonds**
1	**cup sugar**
1	**tablespoon all-purpose flour**
2	**egg whites, lightly beaten**
½	**teaspoon almond extract**

❖ Heat oven to 350°F. Line baking sheets with parchment paper.

❖ In food processor, grind almonds to a powder. In medium bowl, combine almond powder, sugar, flour, egg whites and almond extract; stir until dough forms.

❖ Roll dough by tablespoonfuls into about 20 balls. Arrange about 2 inches apart on lined baking sheets.

❖ Bake about 20 minutes or until lightly browned.

Serves 8.

Preparation time: **5 minutes.**
Ready to serve: **25 minutes.**

Per serving: 425 calories, 19 g total fat (2 g saturated fat), 0 mg cholesterol, 30 mg sodium, 4 g fiber.

DO-AHEAD RECIPE IDEA
Make these cookies the day before and store at room temperature in an airtight container.

INGREDIENTS AND TIPS
Parchment paper is the key to making amaretti that won't stick to the baking sheet.

MOROCCAN MARRAKECH EXPRESS DINNER

Let this menu bring life to the brilliant colors and exotic fragrances of the bazaars and souks (or markets) of Marrakech. All this food is so delicious you may be tempted to eat with your fingers in true Moroccan style.

❖ **Orange and Date Salad**

❖ **Moroccan Carrots**

❖ **Chicken with Lemons and Olives with Couscous**

❖ **Ras el Hanout**

❖ **Preserved Lemons**

❖ **Almond Pastry "Snakes"**

---

for 6

Orange and Date Salad

This salad showcases the best that Morocco has to offer. It is delicious even without the exotic ingredients of orange flower water and Ras el Hanout *(page 104).*

6	**navel oranges**
2	**teaspoons orange flower water (optional)**
½	**cup slivered dates**
½	**cup slivered almonds, toasted**
¼	**cup chopped fresh mint**
1	**teaspoon prepared *Ras el Hanout* (page 104) (optional)**

❖ Peel oranges, removing white pith; section into medium-large bowl. Add orange flower water, if desired; toss to mix.

❖ Arrange orange sections on large serving platter. Sprinkle with dates, almonds, mint and Ras el Hanout, if desired.

Serves 6.

Preparation time: **20 minutes.**
Ready to serve: **20 minutes.**

Per serving: 165 calories, 5.5 g total fat (0.5 g saturated fat), 0 mg cholesterol, 0 mg sodium, 5.5 g fiber.

DO-AHEAD RECIPE IDEA
Oranges can be sectioned the day before and tossed with the orange flower water, then covered and chilled.

INGREDIENTS AND TIPS
Ras el Hanout is a Moroccan spice blend, and like garam masala, changes from spice shop to spice shop and household to household. Cinnamon is a tasty substitute for the blend or you could try making your own using the recipe in this menu.

Orange flower water is an extract made from the petal of the orange blossom.

Moroccan Carrots

These carrots are the perfect accompaniment to Chicken with Lemons and Olives with Couscous (page 102), both in taste and in the lovely color they add to the plate.

1   **lb. carrots, sliced**
2   **tablespoons olive oil**
2   **garlic cloves, minced**
1   **teaspoon whole cumin seeds**

❖ In microwave-safe serving dish, combine carrots and ¼ cup water; cover with plastic wrap. Microwave on High about 4 minutes or just until tender.

❖ Meanwhile, in large skillet, heat oil over medium heat until hot. Add garlic and cumin seeds; sauté about 1 minute or until mixture is fragrant.

❖ Drain carrots. Add carrots to garlic mixture in skillet; cook an additional 1 minute or until carrots are tender and warm.

Serves 6.

Preparation time: **5 minutes.**
Ready to serve: **10 minutes.**

Per serving: 70 calories, 4.5 g total fat (0.5 g saturated fat), 0 mg cholesterol, 25 mg sodium, 2 g fiber.

DO-AHEAD RECIPE IDEA
Prepare this dish the day before and reheat before serving.

INGREDIENTS AND TIPS
Cumin is an herb that originated around the ancient Mediterranean, but which has become popular all over the world.

Chicken with Lemons and Olives with Couscous

This chicken dish delivers a distinctively rich and tangy flavor. It is delicious whether you use fresh lemons or Preserved Lemons (page 104).

3 tablespoons olive oil	1 cup pitted Kalamata olives
12 boneless skinless chicken thighs	2 garlic cloves, minced
2 large onions, sliced	1 tablespoon prepared *Ras el Hanout* (page 104)
2 fresh or preserved lemons, each cut into 8 wedges	2 cups prepared couscous

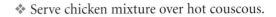

❖ In large saucepan, heat oil over medium-high heat until hot. Add chicken thighs; cook about 2 minutes until browned, turning once.

❖ Add onions, lemons, olives, garlic and Ras el Hanout; mix well. Cover; cook about 20 minutes or until chicken juices run clear.

❖ Serve chicken mixture over hot couscous.

Serves 6.

Preparation time: **10 minutes.**
Ready to serve: **30 minutes.**

Per serving: 385 calories, 18.5 g total fat (4 g saturated fat), 90 mg cholesterol, 440 mg sodium, 4 g fiber.

DO-AHEAD RECIPE IDEA
Prepare this dish the day before and reheat before serving.

INGREDIENTS AND TIPS
Preserved lemons are pickled in salt and lemon juice.

Ras el Hanout

This is a good approximation of the blend that can have as many as 30 spices. It can also contain ground rosebuds if you can get your hands on them.

- **1 tablespoon turmeric**
- **1 tablespoon allspice**
- **1 tablespoon pepper**
- **1 tablespoon ground cinnamon**
- **1 tablespoon nutmeg**
- **2 teaspoons cayenne pepper**

❖ In jar with lid, combine turmeric, allspice, pepper, cinnamon, nutmeg and cayenne pepper; cover tightly. Shake to mix.

Makes about ⅓ cup.

Preparation time: **5 minutes.**
Ready to serve: **5 minutes.**

Per serving: 5 calories, 0 g total fat (0 g saturated fat), 0 mg cholesterol, 0 mg sodium, 0 g fiber.

DO-AHEAD RECIPE IDEA
You can prepare this spice blend ahead of time.

INGREDIENTS AND TIPS
It is best to store this blend and other spices in covered jars in a cool, dry, dark place. This will help preserve the flavors.

Preserved Lemons

These lemons take some time to make. But once you preserve them and place them in the refrigerator, they will last and last.

- **3 lemons, cleaned, each cut into 8 wedges**
- **½ cup kosher (coarse) salt**
- **½ cup lemon juice**
- **Olive oil**

❖ Place lemon wedges in clean 6-cup jar. Add salt and lemon juice; shake gently to mix. Add enough olive oil to cover lemons. Seal jar.

❖ Store in cool, dark place for 7 days, turning jar over each day to distribute juice. Lemons need to be rinsed and pulp removed before using.

Makes 24 wedges.

Preparation time: **7 days.**
Ready to serve: **7 days.**

Per serving: 5 calories, 0.5 g total fat (0 g saturated fat), 0 mg cholesterol, 390 mg sodium, 0 g fiber.

DO-AHEAD RECIPE IDEA
These lemons must be prepared 7 days in advance.

INGREDIENTS AND TIPS
Preserved Lemons will keep for months when sealed and refrigerated.

Almond Pastry "Snakes"

Don't be frightened — these snakes won't hurt you, unless you eat too many of them. If the spiral technique is giving you a problem, cut the rolls into 3-inch lengths and make pastry "sticks."

¾	**cup finely chopped almonds**
¾	**cup sugar**
1	**tablespoon ground cinnamon**
12	**sheets frozen phyllo pastry, thawed**
1	**cup butter, melted**
1	**cup honey**
2	**tablespoons lemon juice**

❖ Heat oven to 350°F.

❖ In medium bowl, combine almonds, sugar and cinnamon; mix well.

❖ Place 1 sheet of phyllo pastry on work surface, keeping remaining sheets covered with damp towel. Brush sheet with melted butter. Fold sheet in half lengthwise. Sprinkle with 2 to 3 tablespoons almond-sugar mixture.

❖ Starting with long side, roll up dough. Coil roll to form spiral "snake"; place on ungreased baking sheet. Brush outside with melted butter. Repeat with remaining pastry sheets and butter.

❖ Bake about 10 minutes or until golden brown. Remove pastries from baking sheet; place on serving platter.

❖ In small microwave-safe bowl, combine honey and lemon juice; mix well. Microwave on High 1 minute. Serve pastries with warm honey syrup.

Serves 6.

Preparation time: **20 minutes.**
Ready to serve: **30 minutes.**

Per serving: 385 calories, 19 g total fat (10 g saturated fat), 40 mg cholesterol, 180 mg sodium, 2 g fiber.

DO-AHEAD RECIPE IDEA

These rolls can be made the day before and refrigerated. Be careful to butter the exterior well and cover with plastic wrap to seal.

INGREDIENTS AND TIPS

Phyllo pastry is paper-thin dough made from flour and water. It is used throughout the Mediterranean for making sweet as well as savory dishes. It is available in the frozen food section of the grocery store.

GREEK DINNER ON THE AEGEAN

The Greeks gave us philosophy and democracy — and a cuisine that celebrates the spectacular and craggy beauty of the Greek islands. The traditional flavors of lemon, lamb, honey and walnut all combine in this neo-classical dinner.

❖ **Lemony Lamb Souvlaki**

❖ **Greek Tsatsiki Yogurt Sauce**

❖ **Saganaki**

❖ **Rustic Greek Salad**

❖ **Honey Walnut Tart**

for 6

Lemon Lamb Souvlaki

Greece is known for its herds of sheep and, of course, its lamb dishes. You can find these lamb kabobs being sold on the streets of almost every Greek city.

2	**lb. boneless lamb, cut into 2-inch cubes**
¼	**cup lemon juice**
¼	**cup olive oil**
2	**garlic cloves, crushed**
2	**teaspoons dried oregano**
⅛	**teaspoon salt**
⅛	**teaspoon freshly ground pepper**
2	**lemons, quartered**
6	**Greek pita folds, heated**

❖ Heat grill.

❖ Place lamb in resealable plastic bag. Add lemon juice, oil, garlic, oregano, and salt and pepper to taste. Seal bag; toss. Marinate at room temperature about 20 minutes.

❖ Thread marinated lamb and lemons onto skewers; reserve marinade.

❖ When ready to grill, place skewers on gas grill over medium heat, on charcoal grill 4 to 6 inches from medium coals or in grill pan. Cook 4 minutes, basting frequently with reserved marinade. Turn and cook an additional 2 to 4 minutes.

❖ Serve lamb with warm pita breads and *Greek Tsatsiki Yogurt Sauce* (page 111).

Serves 6.

Preparation time: **20 minutes.**
Ready to serve: **30 minutes.**

Per serving: 385 calories, 15 g total fat (4 g saturated fat), 100 mg cholesterol, 320 mg sodium, 1 g fiber.

DO-AHEAD RECIPE IDEA
Place the lamb in the marinade and refrigerate the night before.

INGREDIENTS AND TIPS
The lemon is a prominent ingredient in Greek cooking. It is used to flavor sauces, soups, marinades, dressing and, last but not least, dessert.

Greek Tsatsiki Yogurt Sauce

Pour this great sauce over fish, lamb or greens. You can also use it as a dip, plunging in wedges of pita bread or vegetables.

1	**(8-oz.) container plain yogurt (1 cup)**
½	**cup slivered red onion**
¼	**cup chopped fresh mint**
⅛	**teaspoon salt**
⅛	**teaspoon freshly ground pepper**

❖ In medium bowl, combine yogurt, onion and mint; mix well. Season with salt and pepper. Serve immediately, or cover and refrigerate until serving time.

Serves 6.

Preparation time: 15 minutes.
Ready to serve: 15 minutes.

Per serving: 30 calories, 0.5 g total fat (0.5 g saturated fat), 0 mg cholesterol, 30 mg sodium, 0 g fiber.

DO-AHEAD RECIPE IDEA
You can make this sauce the day before.

INGREDIENTS AND TIPS
Yogurt is made from fermented milk. It has a creamy texture and a tangy taste.

Saganaki

Saganaki is not the type of cheese used in this appetizer, but refers to the double-handled skillet in which it is traditionally fried.

12	**oz. Halloumi cheese, cut into ½-inch-thick slices**
4	**tablespoons olive oil**
2	**tablespoons lemon juice**
2	**tablespoons freshly ground pepper**
1	**loaf crusty bread, sliced**

❖ Pat cheese slices dry with paper towels.

❖ In large skillet, heat 2 tablespoons of the oil over medium heat until hot. Add half of the cheese; fry 2 minutes or until golden brown, turning once.

❖ Add more oil to skillet if needed. Repeat with remaining cheese. Arrange cheese on serving platter. Sprinkle with lemon juice and pepper. Serve with bread slices.

Serves 6.

Preparation time: **5 minutes.**
Ready to serve: **5 minutes.**

Per serving: 420 calories, 25 g total fat (10.5 g saturated fat), 50 mg cholesterol, 890 mg sodium, 2.5 g fiber.

DO-AHEAD RECIPE IDEA
The cheese can be sliced ahead, but prepare dish in the last minutes before serving.

INGREDIENTS AND TIPS
Halloumi is a cheese made from ewe's milk. It will fry without melting. Halloumi cheese can be found in specialty cheese shops.

Rustic Greek Salad

There are as many variations of Greek salad as there are villages in Greece. This rustic salad comes from the countryside.

4	medium tomatoes, cut into wedges
1	medium cucumber, peeled, cubed
1	small red onion, thinly sliced
½	cup Kalamata olives, pitted, sliced
8	oz. feta cheese, cubed
¼	cup chopped fresh mint
⅓	cup olive oil
2	tablespoons lemon juice

❖ In large salad bowl, combine tomatoes, cucumber, onion, olives, feta and mint.

❖ In small bowl, combine oil and lemon juice; whisk until well blended. Pour dressing over salad; toss to combine.

Serves 6.

Preparation time: **20 minutes.**
Ready to serve: **20 minutes.**

Per serving: 245 calories, 21.5 g total fat (7.5 g saturated fat), 35 mg cholesterol, 540 mg sodium, 2 g fiber.

DO-AHEAD RECIPE IDEA
The vegetables can be prepared ahead and refrigerated until ready to toss.

INGREDIENTS AND TIPS
Feta cheese is a soft white goat cheese ripened in brine. It has a sharp and salty taste.

Honey Walnut Tart

The best Greek desserts are sweetened with — or drenched in — honey. This melt-in-your-mouth tart follows the tradition to perfection.

1	refrigerated pie crust (from 15-oz. pkg.)
2	eggs
½	cup sugar
½	cup honey
2	tablespoons unsalted butter, melted
¼	teaspoon salt
3	tablespoons anisette (optional)
1	cup chopped walnuts

❖ Heat oven to 400°F.

❖ Press pie crust into 9-inch tart pan; trim excess dough. Bake 10 minutes or until light golden brown. Cool on wire rack. Reduce oven temperature to 375°F.

❖ Meanwhile, in medium bowl, beat eggs until frothy. Add sugar, honey, butter, salt and anisette, if desired; mix well. Stir in walnuts. Pour into partially baked crust.

❖ Bake tart about 20 minutes or until top is dark brown. Cool tart on wire rack 5 minutes. Filling will set as tart cools. Serve warm or cold.

Serves 6.

Preparation time: **10 minutes.**
Ready to serve: **30 minutes.**

Per serving: 465 calories, 24.5 g total fat (5.5 g saturated fat), 80 mg cholesterol, 260 mg sodium, 1.5 g fiber.

DO-AHEAD RECIPE IDEA
This pie can be made the day before.

INGREDIENTS AND TIPS
Anisette is licorice-flavored liquor. You can substitute 1 teaspoon crushed anise seeds if you like.

JAPANESE PARICIPATION DINNER

Simple, pure, elegant, healthful and refreshing are the words most often used to describe tra-ditional Japanese cuisine. Shabu-Shabu *(page 118)* is a dish that epitomizes the eating style known as nabemono. *These dishes are intend-ed to be cooked and eaten with friends around a table, for companionship and warmth in winter.*

❖ **Shabu-Shabu Simmered Beef and Vegetables**

❖ **Sesame Dipping Sauce**

❖ **Crab and Cucumber Salad**

❖ **Edamame**

❖ **Sweet Persimmons with Saki**

for 4

Shabu-Shabu Simmered Beef and Vegetables

This dish, which might be called a Japanese fondue, is named for the sound the beef makes as it is moved back and forth in the broth. In English, this dish might be called "Swish-Swish."

1   lb. beef top loin steak (New York, Kansas City or strip steak), thinly sliced
1   small head Napa cabbage, cored, cut into bite-size pieces
3   carrots, thinly sliced
8   green onions, cut into 2-inch pieces
1   (12-oz.) pkg. firm tofu, cubed
8   cups chicken broth
2   slices fresh ginger
4   cups cooked rice

❖ Divide and arrange steak, cabbage, carrots and onions onto 4 dinner plates.

❖ In electric skillet in center of table, heat chicken broth and ginger over medium heat until hot.

❖ Each place setting should have plate of steak and vegetables, bowl of rice, bowl of *Sesame Dipping Sauce* (page 119) and fondue forks or chopsticks for cooking and dipping. Guests cook their own food, then dip in the sauce and place on rice.

❖ When all food is cooked, cooking broth can be consumed as soup.

Serves 4.

Preparation time: **30 minutes.**
Ready to serve: **30 minutes.**

Per serving: 645 calories, 20 g total fat (5 g saturated fat), 65 mg cholesterol, 2280 mg sodium, 7 g fiber.

DO-AHEAD RECIPE IDEA
Prepare steak and vegetables the day before, cover tightly with plastic wrap and refrigerate.

INGREDIENTS AND TIPS
Tofu is a curd made from soybeans. It comes formed in cakes of varying firmness. It is usually found in the dairy section of grocery stores.

Sesame Dipping Sauce

Use this sauce for dipping with Shabu-Shabu Simmered Beef and Vegetables *(page 118).*

½	**cup tahini**
¼	**cup Japanese soy sauce**
3	**tablespoons sugar**
3	**tablespoons rice vinegar**

❖ In medium bowl, combine tahini, soy sauce, sugar and vinegar; whisk until blended.

Serves 4.

Preparation time: **5 minutes.**
Ready to serve: **5 minutes.**

Per serving: 225 calories, 16 g total fat (2 g saturated fat), 0 mg cholesterol, 1065 mg sodium, 3 g fiber.

DO-AHEAD RECIPE IDEA
The dipping sauce can be made the day before.

INGREDIENTS AND TIPS
Tahini is a paste made from ground sesame seeds and is available in many grocery stores, or Asian or Middle Eastern markets.

Crab and Cucumber Salad

This salad is one of the oldest written recipes in Japanese cuisine and it is as popular today as it was centuries ago!

2	**tablespoons rice vinegar**
1	**tablespoon sugar**
1	**tablespoon mirin**
1	**tablespoon Japanese soy sauce**
2	**cucumbers, peeled, thinly sliced**
1	**(6.5-oz.) can crabmeat, drained**

❖ In small bowl, combine vinegar, sugar, mirin and soy sauce; whisk to blend.

❖ In medium bowl, combine cucumbers and crabmeat. Pour dressing over salad; toss gently to combine.

Serves 4.

Preparation time: **10 minutes.**
Ready to serve: **10 minutes.**

Per serving: 80 calories, 1 g total fat (0 g saturated fat), 40 mg cholesterol, 415 mg sodium, 1 g fiber.

DO-AHEAD RECIPE IDEA
This salad can be prepared earlier in the day.

INGREDIENTS AND TIPS
Mirin is sweet Japanese cooking wine. Japanese soy sauce, which is also called *shoyu,* has a delicate taste and a light color. These ingredients are available in the international aisle of many grocery stores or in Asian markets.

Edamame

Edamame pods contain soybeans that are as addictive as peanuts. The pods are also fun to eat: Just pull the pod through your teeth to pop the beans into your mouth.

2   tablespoons salt
1   (16-oz.) pkg. frozen edamame

❖ Fill large pot with water and 1 tablespoon of the salt. Bring to a boil. Add edamame; cook, uncovered, about 5 minutes.

❖ Drain edamame. Toss with remaining 1 tablespoon salt.

Serves 4.

Preparation time: **5 minutes.**
Ready to serve: **5 minutes.**

Per serving: 80 calories, 3 g total fat (1 g saturated fat), 0 mg cholesterol, 440 mg sodium, 7 g fiber.

DO-AHEAD RECIPE IDEA
You can cook these beans earlier in the day.

INGREDIENTS AND TIPS
Edamame are soybeans in the pod. They are available in the frozen food section of many grocery stores or in Asian markets.

Sweet Persimmons with Saki

Fruit is the dessert of choice in Japan, because it is simple to prepare and because its classic, pure tastes reflect the flavors in the rest of a Japanese menu. Here, substitute mirin for saki, if necessary.

6 ripe persimmons
3 tablespoons saki

❖ Carefully peel persimmons. Cut into 1-inch cubes; place in medium bowl.

❖ Add saki; toss to coat.

Serves 4.

Preparation time: **10 minutes.**
Ready to serve: **10 minutes.**

Per serving: 195 calories, 0.5 g total fat (0 g saturated fat), 0 mg cholesterol, 3.5 mg sodium, 9 g fiber.

DO-AHEAD RECIPE IDEA
Prepare the fruit the day before and refrigerate until ready to serve.

INGREDIENTS AND TIPS
Persimmons, a favorite fruit in Japan, are large, orange and acorn shaped. They are mouth-puckering bitter unless ripe and very soft.

SOIRÉE FRANÇAISE

The French consider food one of life's great pleasures. This menu draws from all the regions of France to bring us the delight of excellent food skillfully prepared.

❖ **Kir Royale**

❖ **Wild Mushroom Cups**

❖ **Beet and Roquefort Salad**

❖ **Sole with Aromatic Vegetables en Papillote**

❖ **Tarte Tatin**

for 8

Kir Royale

This elegant cocktail will make your friends feel like they are getting the "royal" treatment. Sparkling apple juice with a splash of berry syrup makes a good nonalcoholic substitute if you are so inclined.

2 **(759-ml) bottles dry Champagne, chilled**
4 **oz. crème de cassis**

❖ For each drink, pour 6 oz. Champagne and ½ oz. crème de cassis into Champagne flute.

Serves 8.

Preparation time: **5 minutes.**
Ready to serve: **5 minutes.**

Per serving: 165 calories, 0 g total fat (0 g saturated fat), 0 mg cholesterol, 15 mg sodium, 0 g fiber.

DO-AHEAD RECIPE IDEA
Chill the Champagne the day before.

INGREDIENTS AND TIPS
Crème de cassis is a French liquor made by combining sugar and blackberries soaked in alcohol.

Wild Mushroom Cups

A few wild mushrooms added to less expensive domestic ones give a very distinct flavor without a huge expense.

24   slices fine-grained white bread
⅓   cup butter, melted
⅛   cup minced onion
10   oz. mixed wild and domestic mushrooms, coarsely chopped
¼   cup freshly grated Parmesan cheese
⅛   cup sour cream
⅛   teaspoon salt
⅛   teaspoon freshly ground pepper

❖ Heat oven to 400°F.

❖ With 1½-inch round cutter, cut round from each bread slice. Flatten rounds with rolling pin.

❖ In large skillet, reserve 2 tablespoons of the melted butter; set aside. Brush remaining butter on both sides of each bread round. Gently press rounds into miniature muffin cups.

❖ Bake about 10 minutes or until browned.

❖ Meanwhile, add onion to reserved butter in skillet; cook over medium heat about 3 minutes or until tender, stirring frequently. Add mushrooms; cook about 5 minutes or until browned.

❖ Remove skillet from heat. Cool mushroom mixture slightly. Stir in 2 tablespoons of the Parmesan cheese and sour cream. Season with salt and pepper. Spoon mushroom mixture into warm toast cups. Sprinkle with remaining 2 tablespoons Parmesan.

Serves 8.

Preparation time: **10 minutes.**
Ready to serve: **30 minutes.**

Per serving: 140 calories, 11 g total fat (7 g saturated fat), 30 mg cholesterol, 210 mg sodium, 1 g fiber.

DO-AHEAD RECIPE IDEA
Make the bread cups and mushroom mixture the day before. The mushroom mixture can be thoroughly heated and filled just before serving.

INGREDIENTS AND TIPS
Wild mushrooms may not be wild anymore. The varieties that were once hunted in the wild are now farmed. But they still offer distinct flavors.

Beet and Roquefort Salad

This beautiful salad tastes as good as it looks. Beet and Roquefort Salad *offers the added benefit of using the leftover bread scraps from the toast cups in the* Wild Mushroom Cups *(page 127).*

2   **tablespoons butter**
2   **cups cubed bread (¼ inch)**
8   **cups fresh baby spinach leaves**
1   **(15-oz.) can sliced beets, drained**
1   **cup chopped red onion**
1   **cup crumbled Roquefort cheese**
½   **cup olive oil**

❖ In large skillet, melt butter over medium heat. Add bread cubes; cook and stir about 2 minutes or until lightly browned and toasted.

❖ To assemble each salad, place 1 cup spinach on individual salad plate. Top evenly with sliced beets, onion, Roquefort cheese and bread cubes.

❖ Drizzle 1 tablespoon oil over top of each.

Serves 8.

Preparation time: **10 minutes.**
Ready to serve: **10 minutes.**

Per serving: 260 calories, 22 g total fat (7 g saturated fat), 20 mg cholesterol, 400 mg sodium, 3 g fiber.

DO-AHEAD RECIPE IDEA
You can assemble this salad earlier in the day.

INGREDIENTS AND TIPS
Roquefort is a premium French blue cheese. Substitute an American blue cheese if you wish.

Sole with Aromatic Vegetables en Papillote

En papillote means cooking in parchment paper. This ensures that your fish will be moist — and that all the wonderful cooking aromas will be there when you open the paper at the table.

10	**tablespoons butter**
4	**carrots, cut into matchstick-size strips (2x⅛x⅛-inch)**
2	**medium leeks, cut into matchstick-size strips (2x⅛x⅛-inch)**
8	**(12-inch-square) sheets parchment paper**
8	**sole fillets**
8	**sprigs fresh thyme**
⅛	**teaspoon salt**
⅛	**teaspoon freshly ground pepper**

❖ Heat oven to 425°F.

❖ In large skillet, melt 2 tablespoons of the butter over medium heat. Add carrots and leeks; sauté about 2 minutes or until soft.

❖ Fold each sheet of parchment paper in half; cut into half-heart shape. Open papers; place 1 sole fillet on one side of center fold of each. Top each with ⅛ of vegetables, 1 tablespoon remaining butter, 1 thyme sprig, salt and pepper.

❖ Fold untopped side of paper over vegetables. Starting at one end, fold paper and create many tiny folds to seal each packet tight. Place packets on baking sheet.

❖ Bake 15 minutes or until fish flakes easily with a fork.

❖ To serve, let guests open their own packages.

Serves 8.

Preparation time: **15 minutes.**
Ready to serve: **30 minutes.**

Per serving: 275 calories, 13.5 g total fat (7.5 g saturated fat), 120 mg cholesterol, 230 mg sodium, 2 g fiber.

DO-AHEAD RECIPE IDEA
The vegetables can be cut into matchstick-size strips the day before and stored in a covered container until ready to sauté.

INGREDIENTS AND TIPS
Parchment paper is an asset in the kitchen. Nothing will stick to it, and pans lined with it need no washing.

Tarte Tatin

No one is certain how this upside-down apple pie came into being. Legend has it that the Tatin sisters were rushing to make apple pies, and put the apples in the pan before the pastry. To save the pie, they put the pastry crust on top instead of on the bottom. Voilà! The Tarte Tatin *was created.*

1	**cup sugar**
4	**medium Golden Delicious apples, peeled, halved and sliced**
1	**refrigerated pie crust (from 15-oz. pkg.)**
1	**pint French vanilla ice cream**

❖ Heat oven to 375°F.

❖ In large ovenproof skillet, cook sugar over medium heat until golden to caramel in color, stirring frequently.

❖ Place apple slices in skillet; cook about 5 minutes or until barely tender, gently turning slices.

❖ Place pie crust over top of apples; gently tuck crust around apples.

❖ Bake 15 to 20 minutes or until crust is golden brown and apples are tender. Remove from oven; cool tart slightly in skillet. Invert skillet onto serving platter. Serve tart with ice cream.

Serves 8.

Preparation time: **10 minutes.**
Ready to serve: **30 minutes.**

Per serving: 280 calories, 9 g total fat (3.5 g saturated fat), 15 mg cholesterol, 130 mg sodium, 1.5 g fiber.

DO-AHEAD RECIPE IDEA
Make the tart the day before, then heat before serving.

INGREDIENTS AND TIPS
Golden Delicious apples are good for baking because they are not too sweet and they retain their shape. They are also available year-round.

BAJA MEXICAN BARBECUE

Open flame cooking is the world's oldest cooking method, and in Mexico it is an art form. Hearty flavors and simple preparation make this barbecue a festive but casual way to entertain.

❖ **Grilled Steak and Vegetable Fajitas**

❖ **Cilantro Cabbage Slaw**

❖ **Spicy Grilled Corn on the Cob**

❖ **Honey Grilled Pineapple**

❖ **Cajeta Caramel Sauce**

---

for 6

Grilled Steak and Vegetable Fajitas

This is a popular dish in northern Mexico. It is traditionally made with skirt steak, but flank steak makes a good alternative.

2   onions, cut into thick slices
2   bell peppers, stems removed, cut into 4 large slices
3   tablespoons vegetable oil
2   lb. beef skirt or flank steak
1   (1.4-oz.) pkg. fajita seasoning
12   (7-inch) flour tortillas, divided into 2 stacks, wrapped in foil

❖ Heat grill.

❖ In large bowl, combine onions and bell peppers. Add oil; toss to coat.

❖ Place onions and bell peppers on gas grill over medium heat or on charcoal grill about 4 inches from medium coals. Cook about 15 minutes or until golden brown and tender, turning once.

❖ Rub flank steak with fajita seasoning. Place steak on grill; cook 6 to 8 minutes or until nicely browned, turning once. Remove steak from grill; loosely cover with aluminum foil. Let stand about 5 minutes.

❖ Place tortilla packets off to one side of grill away from direct heat. Cook about 5 minutes or until thoroughly heated, turning once.

❖ Remove vegetables from grill. Cut vegetables into bite-size pieces. Cut steak across grain into thin slices. Serve steak and vegetables with warm tortillas.

Serves 6.

Preparation time: **10 minutes.**
Ready to serve: **25 minutes.**

Per serving: 530 calories, 22 g total fat (6 g saturated fat), 80 mg cholesterol, 915 mg sodium, 3 g fiber.

DO-AHEAD RECIPE IDEAS
Vegetables can be prepared earlier in the day.

INGREDIENTS AND TIPS
Skirt steak has an elastic membrane that should be trimmed before grilling. If skirt steak is not available, flank steak is a good substitute.

Cilantro Cabbage Slaw

Put away the grater! The advent of shredded cabbage in a package makes this a fast and easy side dish.

1	**(16-oz.) pkg. coleslaw mix**
6	**green onions, chopped**
1	**cup chopped fresh cilantro**
1	**lime**
3	**tablespoons vegetable oil**
2	**tablespoons honey**

❖ In large salad bowl, combine coleslaw mix, green onions and cilantro.

❖ Grate peel from lime; squeeze juice from lime.

❖ In small bowl, combine lime peel, lime juice, oil and honey; beat with wire whisk until well blended. Pour dressing over salad; toss to combine.

Serves 6.

Preparation time: **10 minutes.**
Ready to serve: **10 minutes.**

Per serving: 125 calories, 9.5 g total fat (1.5 g saturated fat), 0 mg cholesterol, 20 mg sodium, 2 g fiber.

DO-AHEAD RECIPE IDEAS
If you make the coleslaw the day before, the flavors will increase and the cabbage will become nicely wilted.

INGREDIENTS AND TIPS
Cilantro is a very versatile herb. The flavorful leaves and ground seeds are used in dishes around the world.

Spicy Grilled Corn on the Cob

Grilled corn is a treat at many county fairs. But in Mexico, spicy and cheesy grilled corn is a classic street food.

6	**ears corn in husks**
½	**cup mayonnaise**
1	**teaspoon chili powder**
1	**cup grated queso Cotija or freshly grated Parmesan cheese**

❖ Heat grill. Soak corn with husks in cold water 10 minutes.

❖ Remove corn from water; place on gas grill over medium heat or on charcoal grill about 5 inches from medium coals. Cook about 15 minutes or until corn is tender, turning frequently.

❖ Meanwhile, combine mayonnaise and chili powder; blend well. Place cheese on sheet of parchment paper.

❖ Remove husks and silk from corn. Spread mayonnaise mixture over corn; roll in cheese to coat.

Serves 6.

Preparation time: **15 minutes.**
Ready to serve: **30 minutes.**

Per serving: 285 calories, 21 g total fat (6 g saturated fat), 30 mg cholesterol, 240 mg sodium, 2.5 g fiber.

DO-AHEAD RECIPE IDEAS
The corn can be soaked earlier in the day.

INGREDIENTS AND TIPS
Queso Cotija is an aged Mexican cheese that is hard and pungent. Grated Parmesan cheese is a good substitute.

Honey Grilled Pineapple

Buying a ripe and sweet pineapple is easy because of the new sweet varieties available.

**1   pineapple, peeled, cored and cut into
        2-inch chunks**
¼   cup honey

❖ Heat grill. Thread pineapple chunks onto water-soaked bamboo skewers. Brush pineapple with honey.

❖ Place skewered pineapple on gas grill over medium heat or on charcoal grill 4 to 6 inches from medium coals. Cook about 4 minutes or until lightly browned, turning once. Serve pineapple drizzled with *Cajeta Caramel Sauce* (below).

Serves 6.

Preparation time: **5 minutes.**
Ready to serve: **10 minutes.**

Per serving: 80 calories, 0.5 g total fat (0 g saturated fat), 0 mg cholesterol, 1 mg sodium, 1 g fiber.

DO-AHEAD RECIPE IDEAS
The pineapple can be peeled, sliced and cored the day before. The bamboo skewers should be soaked in water for 30 minutes before using to keep them from burning.

INGREDIENTS AND TIPS
To determine whether a pineapple is ripe, try plucking a leaf from the top. If it pulls out readily, it is ripe.

Cajeta Caramel Sauce

This tangy caramel sauce is easy to make and keeps beautifully in the refrigerator. It makes a sensational drizzle for any fruit, ice cream or cake.

**1   (12-oz.) can evaporated goat's or cow's
        milk**
1   cup sugar
2   tablespoons butter
**1   recipe prepared *Honey Grilled
        Pineapple* (above)**

❖ In large saucepan, combine milk, sugar and butter; stir to mix. Cook over medium-high heat 6 to 10 minutes or until mixture comes to a boil, stirring frequently.

❖ Reduce heat; cook an additional 5 to 10 minutes or until sauce becomes caramel in color, stirring frequently. Drizzle sauce over Honey Grilled Pineapple.

Serves 6.

Preparation time: **20 minutes.**
Ready to serve: **20 minutes.**

Per serving: 240 calories, 8 g total fat (5 g saturated fat), 25 mg cholesterol, 85 mg sodium, 0 g fiber.

DO-AHEAD RECIPE IDEAS
The sauce can be made ahead and stored in a covered jar in the refrigerator for about 1 month.

INGREDIENTS AND TIPS
Goat's milk has a tangy taste and is available in a canned evaporated form in many markets or ethnic groceries. Regular evaporated cow's milk can be substituted.

HAVANA HEAT WAVE DINNER

Envision a steamy night in old Havana, with laughter and music in the distance. Cuba's tropical scents and flavors are re-created in these dishes with a definite Latin beat.

❖ **Mini-Cubano Sandwiches**

❖ **Avocado-Orange Salad**

❖ **Arroz con Pollo**

❖ **Mojito Cocktail**

❖ **Buttery Baked Bananas**

for 6

Mini-Cubano Sandwiches

The Cubano may seem like an ordinary ham and cheese sandwich, but the method of cooking here distinguishes it from the ordinary! Grill these sandwiches in a press until they are flattened and the cheese is melted.

3 soft crusted hero-shaped rolls (about 4 oz. each)
1½ tablespoons olive oil
2 tablespoons mustard
6 oz. thinly sliced cooked ham
6 oz. sliced Monterey Jack cheese
6 oz. sweet pickle slices

❖ Cut rolls in half horizontally. Brush top halves with 1 tablespoon of the oil.

❖ Spread bottom halves with mustard. Top evenly with ham, cheese and pickles. Cover with top halves of rolls.

❖ In large skillet, heat remaining ½ tablespoon oil over medium-high heat until hot. Add sandwiches; place heavy weight such as cast-iron skillet on top of sandwiches. Cook 1 to 2 minutes or until bottom is browned. Turn sandwiches; top with weight. Cook an additional 2 minutes.

❖ Cut sandwiches into bite-size pieces. Serve as appetizers.

Serves 6.

Preparation time: **10 minutes.**
Ready to serve: **15 minutes.**

Per serving: 390 calories, 17 g total fat (7 g saturated fat), 45 mg cholesterol, 1245 mg sodium, 2 g fiber.

DO-AHEAD RECIPE IDEA
Sandwiches can be assembled the day before, refrigerated, then grilled at the last minute.

INGREDIENTS AND TIPS
Cuban rolls are soft and chewy. These sandwiches are flattened in a *plancha*, which is a press similar to a waffle iron.

Sandwiches can also be cooked on an indoor hinged grill for half the time.

Avocado-Orange Salad

Sweet oranges, buttery avocados and sharp red onions make a refreshing salad that offers beautiful color as well as wonderful taste.

6	navel oranges, peeled removing pith, cut into slices
2	avocados, pitted, peeled and sliced
½	red onion, thinly sliced
½	cup mayonnaise
¼	cup orange juice
1	tablespoon ground cumin

❖ Arrange orange slices on serving platter. Top with avocado and onion slices.

❖ In small bowl, combine mayonnaise, orange juice and cumin; blend well. Drizzle dressing over salad.

Serves 6.

Preparation time: **15 minutes.**
Ready to serve: **15 minutes.**

Per serving: 300 calories, 24 g total fat (3.5 g saturated fat), 10 mg cholesterol, 110 mg sodium, 7 g fiber.

DO-AHEAD RECIPE IDEA
Oranges and onions can be prepared the day before, along with the dressing. The avocados turn brown so should be prepared at the last minute.

INGREDIENTS AND TIPS
Ripe avocados should yield to gentle pressure. To ripen, place in a loosely closed paper bag at room temperature, and check daily.

Arroz con Pollo

With the help of boneless chicken and frozen vegetables, you can create this classic chicken and rice dish in minutes instead of hours.

2	tablespoons vegetable oil
12	boneless skinless chicken thighs (about 3 oz. each)
1	onion, sliced
1	tablespoon minced garlic
1	cup converted (parboiled) rice
2	(14.5-oz.) cans tomatoes with chiles, undrained

1	(9-oz.) pkg. frozen artichoke hearts, thawed
½	cup pitted green olives
½	cup frozen sweet peas, thawed
⅛	teaspoon salt
⅛	teaspoon freshly ground pepper

❖ In Dutch oven, heat oil over medium-high heat until hot. Add chicken, onion and garlic; cook and stir about 4 minutes or until chicken is browned and onion is tender.

❖ Add rice; cook and stir 1 minute.

❖ Reduce heat to medium. Add tomatoes, artichokes, olives and peas; cover and cook about 25 minutes or until rice is tender. Season with salt and pepper.

Serves 6.

Preparation time: **5 minutes.**
Ready to serve: **30 minutes.**

Per serving: 440 calories, 11 g total fat (3 g saturated fat), 90 mg cholesterol, 815 mg sodium, 5 g fiber.

DO-AHEAD RECIPE IDEA
Prepare this dish earlier in the day and reheat at 325°F until thoroughly hot, about 20 minutes.

INGREDIENTS AND TIPS
Canned tomatoes with chiles can add punch to any dish calling for tomatoes. They have become very popular and are now available in most markets.

Mojito Cocktail

This delicious cocktail is the Cuban version of a mint julep. Crush the mint leaves to release their flavor. For a lighter refreshment, try this combination without the rum.

48	fresh mint leaves
6	tablespoons sugar
12	tablespoons lime juice
12	oz. white rum, chilled
1	quart club soda, chilled

❖ For each cocktail, place 8 mint leaves in tall glass. Add 1 tablespoon sugar; slightly crush mint with back of spoon.

❖ Add 2 tablespoons lime juice and 2 oz. rum. Fill glass with crushed ice. Top with about ⅔ cup club soda or to taste. Stir gently.

Serves 6.

Preparation time: **10 minutes.**
Ready to serve: **10 minutes.**

Per serving: 230 calories, 0 g total fat (0 g saturated fat), 0 mg cholesterol, 40 mg sodium, 0 g fiber.

DO-AHEAD RECIPE IDEA
Crush the mint leaves and assemble the drinks earlier, then add ice and soda at the last minute.

INGREDIENTS AND TIPS
White rum allows the lovely color of the mint leaves to shine.

Buttery Baked Bananas

Bananas aren't just for breakfast. You will love them baked for dessert too. Baking enhances their sweetness and creaminess.

6	**bananas, peeled, cut in half lengthwise and crosswise**
¼	**cup butter**
¼	**cup orange juice**
⅔	**cup packed brown sugar**
1	**teaspoon ground cinnamon**
1	**quart vanilla ice cream**

❖ Heat oven to 350°F.

❖ Arrange bananas in single layer in gratin dish.

❖ In small saucepan, melt butter over medium heat. Stir in orange juice. Pour over bananas. Sprinkle brown sugar and cinnamon evenly over top.

❖ Bake 15 minutes or until thoroughly heated. Serve warm bananas and sauce over ice cream.

Serves 6.

Preparation time: **5 minutes.**
Ready to serve: **20 minutes.**

Per serving: 270 calories, 8 g total fat (5 g saturated fat), 20 mg cholesterol, 60 mg sodium, 3 g fiber.

DO-AHEAD RECIPE IDEA
Assemble this dessert earlier in the day and cook at the last minute.

INGREDIENTS AND TIPS
Contrary to popular belief, ripe bananas can be placed in the refrigerator to keep from going bad. The skin will turn black, but the flesh will be preserved.

GATHERINGS

ENGLISH PUB PARTY

The Public House or "Pub" is a place to meet friends, discuss politics, get a pint and eat authentic British cuisine. You may have heard disparaging comments about English cooking, but once you've tasted these traditional dishes, you're likely to change your mind. Invite friends to play a pub-friendly game of darts and partake of this delicious food with funny names!

- ❖ **Archangels on Horseback**

- ❖ **Scotch Eggs**

- ❖ **Plowman's Platter with Pickled Mushrooms and Onions**

- ❖ **Welsh Rarebit**

- ❖ **Shandy**

- ❖ **Rhubarb Crisp**

for 8

Archangels on Horseback

This is only one of many colorfully named dishes in English cuisine, like Spotted Dick (currant pudding) or Bubble and Squeak (mashed potatoes and cabbage).

16   **medium scallops**
8   **slices bacon, halved**

❖ Heat broiler.

❖ Wrap scallops with half slice of bacon; secure with toothpick. Place on broiler pan.

❖ Broil about 5 minutes or until bacon is crisp and scallops are opaque.

Serves 8.

Preparation time: **5 minutes.**
Ready to serve: **10 minutes.**

Per serving: 30 calories, 1.5 g total fat (0.5 g saturated fat), 5 mg cholesterol, 80 mg sodium, 0 g fiber.

DO-AHEAD RECIPE IDEA
Wrap the scallops the day before. Cover and store in the refrigerator.

INGREDIENTS AND TIPS
The scallops can be replaced with oysters, but then the name of the dish changes to "Angels on Horseback."

Scotch Eggs

In pubs, these eggs are deep-fried. But they are just as tasty and a lot less messy when baked in the oven.

8   **hard-cooked eggs, peeled**
½   **cup all-purpose flour**
1   **lb. seasoned pork sausage**
1   **cup corn flake crumbs**

❖ Heat oven to 400°F.

❖ Coat hard-cooked eggs with flour; shake off excess.

❖ Divide sausage into 8 equal parts; shape each into thin patty. Wrap 1 sausage patty around each egg to cover.

❖ Place crumbs on sheet of parchment paper. Roll sausage-covered eggs in crumbs to coat; place on ungreased baking sheet. Spray eggs with non-stick cooking spray.

❖ Bake about 20 minutes or until sausage is thoroughly cooked and no longer pink. Cool slightly. Cut eggs into quarters to serve.

Serves 8.

Preparation time: **10 minutes.**
Ready to serve: **30 minutes.**

Per serving: 215 calories, 13.5 g total fat (4.5 g saturated fat), 235 mg cholesterol, 465 mg sodium, 0.5 g fiber.

DO-AHEAD RECIPE IDEA
The eggs can be cooked, peeled and wrapped the day before.

INGREDIENTS AND TIPS
Coating the eggs with flour helps the sausage stick to them as they cook. It also helps to dust your hands with flour when wrapping the eggs.

Plowman's Platter with Pickled Mushrooms and Onions

As the name implies, this was once the lunch that farm workers carried into the fields for their midday meal. Now it is a popular businessman's pub lunch.

2	cups fresh mushrooms, halved
¾	cup malt vinegar
½	teaspoon salt
4	oz. Stilton cheese
4	oz. English cheddar cheese
1	small loaf crusty bread, sliced
1	(7-oz.) jar pickled onions, drained

❖ In medium saucepan, combine mushrooms, vinegar and salt; cook over medium heat about 10 minutes, stirring occasionally.

❖ Drain mushrooms; serve immediately, or cool completely, store mushrooms in brine and drain when ready to serve.

❖ Assemble serving platter with Stilton and cheddar cheeses, bread slices, drained mushrooms and pickled onions.

Serves 8.

Preparation time: **10 minutes.**
Ready to serve: **20 minutes.**

Per serving: 240 calories, 10.5 g total fat (6 g saturated fat), 25 mg cholesterol, 615 mg sodium, 2 g fiber.

DO-AHEAD RECIPE IDEA
The mushrooms can be made up to a week before and stored in brine in a covered jar in the refrigerator.

INGREDIENTS AND TIPS
Stilton is called the "king" of English cheese. It is the English variety of blue cheese.

Malt vinegar is on every table in a pub. If you order fish and chips, you want to pour malt vinegar over them. White wine vinegar would make a good substitute.

Welsh Rarebit

Getting real English cheddar is important in this recipe. The processed American variety just does not have the same flavor, nor does it melt as well. Substitute American beer for the ale, if you wish.

8   oz. (2 cups) grated English cheddar
    cheese
½   cup ale
2   tablespoons butter
2   tablespoons English mustard powder
8   slices hearty bread, crusts removed,
    toasted

❖ Heat broiler. Line 15x10x1-inch baking pan with aluminum foil.

❖ In small saucepan, melt cheese, ale and butter over low heat, stirring constantly. Add mustard; stir to blend.

❖ Place toasted bread in foil-lined pan. Pour cheese over bread.

❖ Broil about 2 minutes or until bubbly and browned. Cool toast about 4 minutes or until hardened slightly. Cut each toast into 4 pieces. Serve warm.

Serves 8.

Preparation time: **10 minutes.**
Ready to serve: **20 minutes.**

Per serving: 205 calories, 13.5 g total fat (8 g saturated fat), 35 mg cholesterol, 305 mg sodium, 1.5 g fiber.

DO-AHEAD RECIPE IDEA
Prepare this dish only at the last minute.

INGREDIENTS AND TIPS
English mustard powder is very strong and pungent. Find it in the spice aisle.

Shandy

They serve more than straight ale in pubs! This refreshing beverage is also a popular pub drink. Try it and discover why.

1 **(12-oz.) can frozen lemonade concentrate, thawed**
2 **cups cold water**
8 **cups chilled beer**

❖ In pitcher, combine lemonade concentrate and water; stir to mix.

❖ To serve, pour equal parts of lemonade and beer into large glasses.

Serves 8.

Preparation time: **5 minutes.**
Ready to serve: **5 minutes.**

Per serving: 175 calories, 0 g total fat (0 g saturated fat), 0 mg cholesterol, 15 mg sodium, 1.5 g fiber.

DO-AHEAD RECIPE IDEA
Make the lemonade the day before.

INGREDIENTS AND TIPS
Nonalcoholic beer can be used to make a shandy that still tastes great.

Rhubarb Crisp

This old-fashioned English dessert admirably represents the homey cuisine served in pubs.

1	cup old-fashioned rolled oats
1	cup packed brown sugar
½	cup all-purpose flour
½	cup unsalted butter
4	cups frozen diced rhubarb, thawed, drained
½	cup sugar

❖ Heat oven to 425°F. Spray 8-inch square pan with nonstick cooking spray.

❖ In medium bowl, combine oats, brown sugar and flour; mix well. Cut in butter with a pastry blender until mixture is crumbly.

❖ Spread half of oat mixture in bottom of prepared pan; gently press to form crust. Spread rhubarb evenly over crust. Sprinkle sugar over rhubarb. Top with remaining oat mixture.

❖ Bake about 25 minutes or until rhubarb is tender and topping is crisp and browned. Serve warm.

Serves 8.

Preparation time: **5 minutes.**
Ready to serve: **30 minutes.**

Per serving: 325 calories, 12 g total fat (7 g saturated fat), 30 mg cholesterol, 15 mg sodium, 2 g fiber.

DO-AHEAD RECIPE IDEA
You can make this crisp the day before.

INGREDIENTS AND TIPS
Frozen rhubarb has all the qualities of fresh and it cooks faster.

CHINESE DIM SUM

Dim Sum *means "Heart's Delight" in Cantonese, and the name is well given. The Dim Sum served in the tea houses of southern China include bite-size dumplings, savory pastries and a variety of sweet morsels. Here are just some of the delights you might find in a Dim Sum selection.*

❖ **Shrimp-Stuffed Peppers**

❖ **Zesty Pork Pot Stickers**

❖ **Goyza Dipping Sauce**

❖ **Minced Chicken with Peanuts and Coconut in Lettuce Cups**

❖ **Sweet Ginger Cookies**

for 8

Shrimp-Stuffed Peppers

These are no ordinary stuffed peppers. The shrimp add a seafood twist, the peanut oil and soy give everything that Asian flavor.

1   **lb. shelled, deveined uncooked medium shrimp**
2   **green onions, minced**
3   **small green bell peppers**
2   **tablespoons paprika**
1   **tablespoon peanut oil**
1   **cup chicken broth**
1   **tablespoon soy sauce**
1   **teaspoon cornstarch**

❖ In food processor, combine shrimp and green onions; pulse until shrimp are minced.

❖ Wash and dry outsides of bell peppers before cutting so insides remain dry. Cut bell peppers in half lengthwise; remove core. Cut each half into quarters. Stuff each bell pepper piece with shrimp mixture. Sprinkle each with paprika.

In large skillet, heat oil over medium-high heat until hot. Add stuffed pepper pieces, filling side down; cook about 1 minute or until lightly browned. Turn, filling side up. Add ½ cup of the chicken broth; cook an additional 3 minutes or until shrimp turn pink and bell peppers are thoroughly cooked.

In small bowl, mix remaining ½ cup chicken broth, soy sauce and cornstarch until well blended. Add mixture to skillet; cook and stir 1 minute or until sauce has thickened.

Place stuffed peppers on serving platter. Pour sauce over top.

Serves 8.

Preparation time: **15 minutes.**
Ready to serve: **25 minutes.**

Per serving: 55 calories, 2.5 g total fat (0.5 g saturated fat), 55 mg cholesterol, 200 mg sodium, 0.5 g fiber.

DO-AHEAD RECIPE IDEA
The shrimp mixture can be prepared the day before. The peppers can be stuffed earlier in the day, but only cook them just before serving.

INGREDIENTS AND TIPS
Peanut oil is the preferred oil for Asian cooking. It imparts a nutty flavor to the dish and has a high smoke point for frying.

Zesty Pork Pot Stickers

Pot stickers are a delicious accident. It all started when pork dumplings burned and stuck to the bottom of a pan. The dish was saved when steam released the dumplings. The birth of a new treat!

½	**lb. ground pork**
2	**teaspoons minced fresh ginger**
1	**teaspoon grated orange peel**
1	**egg**
1	**tablespoon soy sauce**
½	**teaspoon garlic-chili sauce**
24	**wonton skins**
2	**tablespoons peanut oil**

❖ In medium bowl, combine ground pork, ginger, orange peel, egg, soy sauce and garlic-chili sauce; mix well. For each pot sticker, place 1 heaping teaspoon pork mixture in center of 1 wonton skin. Moisten edges of wonton skin with water; fold into a triangle and press to seal.

❖ In large skillet, heat 1 tablespoon of the oil over medium-high heat until hot. Add half of the pot stickers; cook about 4 minutes or until pork is no longer pink in center and pot stickers are golden, turning once. Add ¼ cup water to skillet. Immediately cover; reduce heat to medium.

Simmer 5 minutes. Remove pot stickers from skillet; discard water and wipe skillet dry. Repeat with remaining tablespoon oil and remaining half of pot stickers. Serve pot stickers with *Goyza Dipping Sauce* (below).

Serves 8.

Preparation time: **20 minutes.**
Ready to serve: **30 minutes.**

Per serving: 55 calories, 3 g total fat (1 g saturated fat), 20 mg cholesterol, 55 mg sodium, 1 g fiber.

DO-AHEAD RECIPE IDEA
The pork mixture can be made the day before and the dumplings can be assembled earlier in the day.

INGREDIENTS AND TIPS
Wonton skin packages are available in the produce or frozen food section of grocery stores.

Goyza Dipping Sauce

Use this light and delightful sauce as a dip or dressing. Either way, it's easy and fabulous.

½	**cup low-sodium soy sauce**
¼	**cup rice vinegar**
2	**tablespoons sesame oil**

❖ In small bowl, combine soy sauce, vinegar and oil; beat well with whisk.

Serves 8.

Preparation time: **5 minutes.**
Ready to serve: **5 minutes.**

Per serving: 40 calories, 3.5 g total fat (0.5 g saturated fat), 0 mg cholesterol, 600 mg sodium, 0 g fiber.

DO-AHEAD RECIPE IDEA
Make this sauce the day before and refrigerate.

INGREDIENTS AND TIPS
Prepared Goyza sauce is available at Asian markets.

Minced Chicken with Peanuts and Coconut in Lettuce Cups

Cool lettuce leaves wrap around a warm chicken mixture to create a remarkable combination of textures and flavors that every palate will love.

1	tablespoon peanut oil		½	cup chopped salted peanuts
4	green onions, chopped		½	cup flaked coconut
2	garlic cloves, minced		¼	cup oyster sauce
2	tablespoons minced fresh ginger		2	heads Boston lettuce
1	lb. minced chicken or turkey			

- In large skillet, heat oil over medium-high heat until hot. Add green onions, garlic and ginger; cook and stir about 1 minute or until softened.

- Add chicken; cook about 4 minutes or until chicken is no longer pink, stirring frequently.

- Add peanuts, coconut and oyster sauce; mix well. Cook and stir an additional minute or until mixture is thoroughly heated.

- Serve chicken mixture in serving bowl surrounded by lettuce leaves.

Serves 8.

Preparation time: **10 minutes.**
Ready to serve: **15 minutes.**

Per serving: 180 calories, 10 g total fat (3 g saturated fat), 35 mg cholesterol, 425 mg sodium, 2 g fiber.

DO-AHEAD RECIPE IDEA
Make the chicken mixture earlier in the day. Serve warm or at room temperature.

INGREDIENTS AND TIPS
Oyster sauce has a salty, slightly sweet flavor. It is made from oysters and soy sauce, but does not have a fishy taste.

Sweet Ginger Cookies

End this casual party of appetizers with light flavor and style. These Asian-flavored cookies provide the perfect and delicious answer!

1	**cup sugar**
1	**cup shortening**
1	**egg, lightly beaten**
1	**teaspoon vanilla**
1	**teaspoon baking powder**
¼	**teaspoon salt**
¾	**cup finely minced crystallized ginger**
2½	**cups all-purpose flour**

❖ Heat oven to 325°F. Line baking sheets with parchment paper.

❖ In large bowl, beat sugar and shortening with spoon until light and fluffy. Add egg, vanilla, baking powder, salt and ginger; stir to combine. Stir in ½ cup flour at a time until well combined and dough forms.

❖ Using tablespoonfuls of dough, shape into balls. Arrange balls about 2 inches apart on lined baking sheets. Flatten balls.

❖ Bake about 15 minutes or until golden brown. Immediately remove from baking sheets.

Serves 8.

Preparation time: **10 minutes.**
Ready to serve: **25 minutes.**

Per serving: 140 calories, 7 g total fat (2 g saturated fat), 5 mg cholesterol, 50 mg sodium, 0.5 g fiber.

DO-AHEAD RECIPE IDEA
This cookie dough can be made ahead and refrigerated. You can also bake the cookies ahead of time.

INGREDIENTS AND TIPS
Crystallized ginger is gingerroot that has been sliced, preserved in sugar and dried.

MIDNIGHT IN MOSCOW
ZAKUSKI PARTY

Zakuski *translates into "little bites." The zakuski party — the Russian version of our cocktail party — became a popular entertaining venue during the reign of the Czars. The royal families of Russia are long gone, but zakuski parties remain. The appetizers are varied. But since it's a Russian tradition, caviar is a must and vodka is the beverage of choice.*

❖ **Lamb Meatballs with Walnuts and Currants**

❖ **Horseradish Dipping Sauce**

❖ **Shiitake Mushroom Caviar**

❖ **Stuffed Eggs with Caviar**

❖ **Feta and Basil Platter**

---

for 8

Lamb Meatballs with Walnuts and Currants

These unusual meatballs are rich, slightly sweet and a little nutty. Just take one bite and you too will be hooked forever!

1	**lb. ground lamb**
½	**cup finely chopped walnuts**
⅓	**cup dried currants**
¼	**cup chopped green onions**
¼	**cup chopped fresh mint**
1	**egg**
½	**teaspoon salt**
½	**teaspoon allspice**

❖ Heat oven to 400°F. Spray shallow baking pan with nonstick cooking spray.

❖ In large bowl, combine ground lamb, walnuts, currants, green onions, mint, egg, salt and allspice; mix thoroughly.

❖ Shape mixture into 1-inch balls. Arrange in prepared pan.

❖ Bake 10 to 15 minutes or until no longer pink in center. Serve meatballs with *Horseradish Dipping Sauce* (page 175).

Serves 8.

Preparation time: **15 minutes.**
Ready to serve: **30 minutes.**

Per serving: 185 calories, 13 g total fat (4 g saturated fat), 60 mg cholesterol, 180 mg sodium, 0 g fiber.

DO-AHEAD RECIPE IDEA
Make the meatballs the day before and reheat just before serving.

INGREDIENTS AND TIPS
Allspice is seed from a pod that grows on an evergreen tree. It combines the flavors of cinnamon, nutmeg and cloves, which is how it gets its name.

Horseradish Dipping Sauce

Horseradish, a very popular condiment in Russia, makes the perfect accompaniment for the slightly sweet-and-nutty essence of Lamb Meatballs with Walnuts and Currants *(page 174).*

- ½ **cup mayonnaise**
- ⅓ **cup sour cream**
- 3 **tablespoons prepared horseradish**

❖ In medium bowl, combine mayonnaise, sour cream and horseradish; blend well. Serve with *Lamb Meatballs with Walnuts and Currants* (page 174).

Serves 8.

Preparation time: **5 minutes.**
Ready to serve: **5 minutes.**

Per serving: 120 calories, 13 g total fat (3 g saturated fat), 15 mg cholesterol, 90 mg sodium, 0 g fiber.

DO-AHEAD RECIPE IDEA
The sauce can be made the day before.

INGREDIENTS AND TIPS
Horseradish is a long root. It is very hot when grated and eaten raw. It becomes milder when cooked.

Shiitake Mushroom Caviar

In Russia, any spread that is made of minced vegetables is called caviar. *No zakuski or cocktail party would be complete without at least one vegetable caviar!*

3	tablespoons olive oil
8	oz. shiitake mushrooms, stems removed and discarded, chopped
8	oz. white mushrooms, chopped
1	medium onion, chopped
2	garlic cloves, chopped
3	tablespoons mayonnaise
2	tablespoons chopped fresh dill
1/8	teaspoon salt
1/8	teaspoon freshly ground pepper
	Russian black bread triangles or crackers

❖ In large skillet, heat oil over medium heat until hot. Add mushrooms, onion and garlic; cook, stirring occasionally, 12 to 15 minutes or until vegetables are browned and no liquid remains.

❖ Place mixture in food processor; pulse to mince. Place mixture in medium bowl.

❖ Add mayonnaise and dill; mix well. Season with salt and pepper. Serve with bread triangles or crackers.

Serves 8.

Preparation time: **10 minutes.**
Ready to serve: **25 minutes.**

Per serving: 100 calories, 9.5 g total fat (1.5 g saturated fat), 5 mg cholesterol, 30 mg sodium, 0 g fiber.

DO-AHEAD RECIPE IDEA
You can make this mushroom caviar the day before and refrigerate it.

INGREDIENTS AND TIPS
Shiitake mushrooms have a rich, smoky flavor. They are now farmed, which makes them more available in grocery stores. The stems are extremely tough and should always be discarded. White mushrooms can be substituted for the shiitakes.

Stuffed Eggs with Caviar

A topping of real caviar makes these simple stuffed eggs absolutely extraordinary.

1   **(4-oz.) jar caviar**
8   **hard-cooked eggs, cooled, peeled and halved**
¼   **cup sour cream**
2   **tablespoons chopped fresh chives**

❖ Place caviar in fine strainer. Rinse thoroughly with cold water to refresh. Set aside.

❖ Gently remove egg yolks from egg halves, leaving egg whites intact; place yolks in medium bowl.

❖ Mash yolks with fork. Add sour cream and chives; stir to combine.

❖ Fill egg white halves with yolk mixture, mounding slightly. Top each with 1 teaspoon caviar.

Serves 8.

Preparation time: **15 minutes.**
Ready to serve: **15 minutes.**

Per serving: 125 calories, 9 g total fat (3 g saturated fat), 300 mg cholesterol, 280 mg sodium, 0 g fiber.

DO-AHEAD RECIPE IDEA
Cook the eggs and make the filling the day before. Stuff the eggs just before serving.

INGREDIENTS AND TIPS
Here, caviar is fish roe or eggs. Roe from the Caspian sturgeon is highly prized and very expensive. Salmon or whitefish roe is much more available and affordable.

Feta and Basil Platter

Feta cheese is stored in brine and can be very salty. Soak it in cold water to remove some of the salt.

½	**lb. feta cheese, sliced**
1	**tablespoon red wine vinegar**
¼	**cup olive oil**
½	**teaspoon Hungarian paprika**
2	**oz. fresh basil, shredded**
24	**rye bread triangles, toasted**

❖ Arrange feta cheese slices on serving platter.

❖ In small bowl, whisk vinegar, oil and paprika until well blended. Drizzle mixture over cheese. Sprinkle with basil. Serve with rye bread triangles.

Serves 8.

Preparation time: **10 minutes.**
Ready to serve: **10 minutes.**

Per serving: 185 calories, 13.5 g total fat (5 g saturated fat), 25 mg cholesterol, 445 mg sodium, 0 g fiber.

DO-AHEAD RECIPE IDEA
Assemble the cheese platter the day before. But, add the basil only at the last minute.

INGREDIENTS AND TIPS
Hungarian paprika is ground, dried, hot red peppers. Paprika can also be made from sweet red peppers. Paprika from Hungarian peppers is considered the best.

INTERNATIONAL SOUP SUMMIT

Soup is the universal comfort food. Whether thick and hearty or light and creamy, it satisfies and warms. Entertain friends and family with large pots of soup, loaves of bread and platters of cheese. It is the perfect meal to accompany an evening of board games, ice hockey, family videos — any gathering.

❖ **Moroccan Lamb-Chickpea Soup**

❖ **Greek Egg-Lemon Soup**

❖ **Cuban Shrimp Soup**

❖ **German Sauerkraut and Sausage Soup**

---

for 8

Moroccan Lamb-Chickpea Soup

Muslims often serve this hearty soup to break the fast at sundown in the holy month of Ramadan.

½   **lb. ground lamb**
1   **large onion, chopped**
4   **cups beef broth**
1   **(28-oz.) can pureed tomatoes**
1   **(15-oz.) can chickpeas, drained**
1   **cup chopped fresh cilantro**
1   **tablespoon curry powder**

❖ In large soup pot, cook ground lamb and onion over medium-high heat about 3 minutes or until lamb is browned and onion is soft, stirring frequently.

❖ Add beef broth, tomatoes, chickpeas, cilantro and curry powder. Reduce heat; simmer about 20 minutes or until flavors are blended.

Serves 8.

Preparation time: **5 minutes.**
Ready to serve: **25 minutes.**

Per serving: 170 calories, 5 g total fat (2 g saturated fat), 20 mg cholesterol, 1010 mg sodium, 4.5 g fiber.

DO-AHEAD RECIPE IDEA
This soup will taste even better if made the day before and reheated before serving.

INGREDIENTS AND TIPS
Chickpeas, also called garbanzo beans, are versatile legumes. They are native to the Middle East, but are used all around the world.

Greek Egg-Lemon Soup

This soup is as light and delicate as the other soups are hearty. Jasmine rice cooks more quickly than long-grain rice, and adds a subtle flavor to the soup.

8	cups chicken broth
⅔	cup jasmine rice
6	eggs
½	cup lemon juice
1	lemon, sliced

❖ In large soup pot, cook chicken broth and rice over medium heat about 15 minutes or until broth is hot and rice is tender.

❖ Meanwhile, in medium bowl, whisk eggs until well blended. Whisk in lemon juice.

❖ Add about ½ cup hot broth, stirring constantly, to egg-lemon mixture.

❖ Add egg-lemon mixture to rice mixture; cook about 2 minutes, stirring constantly. Do not let soup boil or egg mixture will curdle. Serve soup garnished with lemon slices.

Serves 8.

Preparation time: **5 minutes.**
Ready to serve: **25 minutes.**

Per serving: 155 calories, 5.5 g total fat (1.5 g saturated fat), 160 mg cholesterol, 1090 mg sodium, 0.5 g fiber.

DO-AHEAD RECIPE IDEA
Start the chicken broth and rice earlier in the day. Prepare the egg-lemon mixture and add just before finishing the soup.

INGREDIENTS AND TIPS
Frozen pure lemon juice provides the flavor of fresh lemons without the work of juicing.

For the best flavor, only make this soup with fresh squeezed or frozen fresh juice.

Cuban Shrimp Soup

Surprisingly, it is the shells of the shrimp that provide the intense shrimp flavor to the soup stock here.

1	**lb. shrimp with shells**
3	**tablespoons butter**
2	**cups water**
6	**small new red potatoes, diced**
1	**large onion, chopped**
2	**garlic cloves, minced**
2	**(12-oz.) cans evaporated milk**
1	**(14.5-oz.) can diced tomatoes, drained**
2	**cups whole kernel corn**

❖ Remove shells from shrimp. Set shrimp aside.

❖ In medium saucepan, melt 1 tablespoon of the butter over high heat. Add shells; sauté about 1 minute. Add water; bring to a boil. Boil about 10 minutes or until water is reduced to about 1 cup.

❖ Meanwhile, in large soup pot, melt remaining 2 tablespoons butter over medium heat. Add potatoes, onion and garlic; sauté about 5 minutes or until tender.

❖ Add shrimp, evaporated milk, tomatoes, corn and shrimp stock made from shells; mix well. Reduce heat; simmer 15 minutes.

Serves 8.

Preparation time: **15 minutes.**
Ready to serve: **30 minutes.**

Per serving: 265 calories, 11.5 g total fat (6.5 g saturated fat), 90 mg cholesterol, 270 mg sodium, 2.5 g fiber.

DO-AHEAD RECIPE IDEA
This soup can be made the day before and heated thoroughly before serving.

INGREDIENTS AND TIPS
Evaporated milk is a staple in countries with hot climates, where fresh milk is not always available.

German Sauerkraut and Sausage Soup

This soup is everything that comes to mind when you think of German cooking — robust, flavorful and very substantial.

4   slices bacon, diced
2   medium potatoes, diced
1   large onion, chopped
6   oz. smoked sausage, sliced
1   (16-oz.) can sauerkraut, drained, rinsed
6   cups beef broth
2   tablespoons tomato paste
2   teaspoons caraway seeds

❖ In large soup pot, cook bacon, potatoes and onion over medium heat about 5 minutes or until potatoes and onion are soft.

❖ Add sausage, sauerkraut, beef broth, tomato paste and caraway seeds. Reduce heat; simmer about 15 minutes or until flavors are blended.

Serves 8.

Preparation time: **10 minutes.**
Ready to serve: **30 minutes.**

Per serving: 185 calories, 12 g total fat (4.5 g saturated fat), 15 mg cholesterol, 645 mg sodium, 2.5 g fiber.

DO-AHEAD RECIPE IDEA
Make this soup the day before. It only gets better with reheating!

INGREDIENTS AND TIPS
Sauerkraut has a bad reputation for being too sour and pungent. Actually, these bad traits disappear when it is rinsed under cold water before using; this is how sauerkraut was always meant to be used.

RECIPE INDEX

GENERAL INDEX